John R. Daniels

The Psychic Nerd

A True Story

Copyright @ 2015 John R.Daniels. All rights reserved

No part of this book may be produced in any written, electronic, recording or photocopying without written permission of the publisher or author. The exception would be in the case of brief quotations embodied in the critical articles or reviews and pages where permission is specifically granted by the publisher or author.

ISBN: 978-0-9942732-0-8

First Edition

Printed in Australia

To contact the author

Johnrdaniels_tpn@outlook.com

Or follow on Twitter at @thepsychicnerd

Acknowledgements

To my wonderful wife and son for all their support whilst I was writing this book; from the original idea of putting my experiences to paper and the final completion of this book I am eternally grateful and love you both forever.

To all the people who have helped me in understanding my skills over the years and aided me in my development I will always be grateful for your understanding and teaching.

Table of Contents

Chapter 1 – What's It All About?

Chapter 2 – The Beginning – Mind Your Head

Chapter 3 – Feeling A Presence

Chapter 4 – Seeking Solace in Religion

Chapter 5 – The Jester

Chapter 6 – Asteroids

Chapter 7 – Now Get Out

Chapter 8 – Growing Up

Chapter 9 - Heart Breaking News

Chapter 10 – The Tutor

Chapter 11 – Learning The Ropes

Chapter 12 – Life Changing

Chapter 13 – Shadow Visitors

Chapter 14 – Leave Him Alone

Chapter 15 – The Hangers

Chapter 16 – Rachel's Friend

Chapter 17 – Cirencester Hotel Visitor

Chapter 18 – The Dancing Bar

Chapter 19 – Jamaica

Chapter 20 – Street Psychic

Chapter 21 – Man's Best Friend

Chapter 22 – The Fridge

Chapter 23 – You Reap What You Sow

Chapter 24 – A Christmas Carol

Chapter 25 – Angels

Chapter 26 – The Last Lift

Chapter 27 – The Peaceful Hour

Chapter 28 – New Beginnings

Chapter 29 – A Friend Comes Calling

Chapter 30 – Dark Forces

Chapter 31 – They Just Push Through

Chapter 32 – The Young Girl

Chapter 33 – Unwanted Guests

Chapter 34 – Spooks On The Barbie

Chapter 35 – The Gypsy & Reiki Healer

Chapter 36 – We Are Still Here

Chapter 37 – Meditation Without Wings

Chapter 38 – Positive Uses

Chapter 39 – Tower Of London

Chapter 40 – Coffee Confirmation

Chapter 41 – Family Comes Calling

Chapter 42 – What Are You Waiting For

Chapter 43 – Crayons

Chapter 44 – General Beliefs

Chapter 45 – Where To Now

Chapter 1

What's It's All About?

The Psychic Nerd

This book is the story of my life up to this point, I have written this book to give people an insight into my life which has been far from ordinary as you will realize.

All of what you are about to read is completely true, and all narratives depicted have actually happened to me personally and continue to be experienced up to the present day. These experiences have often been experienced in the company of other people.

Each chapter portrays a clear and precise description of all events that have unfolded without any elaborate descriptions or embellishment of the truth in order to make the story more attractive or dramatic. However to protect the privacy of people throughout this book their names have been changed.

I would like to point out that what you are about to read is not always accepted by some people, understandably some people are skeptical and often ridicule matters they have no understanding of. I hope this book gives you a greater insight into what some people live through and experience on a daily basis. I can assure you that all of this happened to me and I continue to encounter to this day.

My name is Robert Daniels; I am the wrong side of 40 and currently live in Australia after emigrating from the UK in 2007 with my wonderful wife Helen and teenage son Lucas. I currently work in the IT industry and I have been working in this field for over 30 years. My chosen career has required on a daily basis the analysis, design and development of many computer systems and applications. This type of work involves a considerable amount of logical and analytical thinking; I have applied the same logic outside of the IT industry when encountering a lot of what you will read within this book.

Before we continue any further I would like to address the title of this book, my other skills apart from I.T. career are difficult to categorize, the easiest way I can describe them is that of a psychic medium. However I will let you determine what they are when you have finished reading this book.

I had the notion to write this book in late 2012 and some 8-9 months later, with the support and encouragement from my closest family and friends, I finally took the formidable first steps in starting to "put pen to paper".

My main reason for wanting to write this book is to illustrate to people that there are manifestations far beyond our realms of normal expectations around us all the time; some people are privileged enough to sense and recognize them when they happen. This is often referred to as a sixth sense; personally I think there are a lot more than six senses.

Most of us sense things using sight, sound or smell and since I was a young child I have found I can also smell, feel, see and hear happenings not noticeable to other people. These skills range from seeing auras, picking up on peoples' feelings, seeing shadows around people and receiving messages about these peoples. I can also travel in my mind very quickly to a location connected to whoever I am talking to or talking about with quite accurate detail literally within seconds of meeting or speaking to people. I can also detect and feel spirits around me in buildings or locations that I visit. Believe me when I say it has taken me a considerable amount of time for me to recognize and acknowledge these skills and it has taken me a long time to develop my abilities from the fundamental abilities I had as a child right up to early adulthood.

As I stated earlier I had the initial inkling for this book for almost a year before I finally decided to put pen to paper. I do often have many ideas for various schemes and unfortunately tend not to see many of them through to fruition. However all things changed for me a couple of months prior to starting this book. I kept remembering a phrase I had read somewhere that stated 'if you always do what you have always done then you will always get what you have already got'. My interpretation of this was that if I truly wanted to make a change in my life I had to make a stand, make important changes in my life otherwise the status quo would remain. Don't get me wrong I understand that it's not always easy to make significant changes due to family life and working commitments but it was time to make a start. So I started trying to complete some I.T. work I had always thought about developing but along the way two events happened which changed the path I would eventually take.

The first incident was a sudden and severe illness that literally took the wind out of my sails having always previously been fit and healthy up to this point. Following two months of severe pain, debility, numerous medical investigations and appointments with physicians, I found myself lying in an MRI machine undergoing a brain scan. At this point, slowly gliding through this huge, claustrophobic, noisy machine, I made a promise to myself that if I was given a clean bill of health I would start moving forward, no more excuses. Thankfully the result was good news and I began on my road to recovery.

The second incident, just a couple of weeks later, was during a visit to a local spiritual church meeting. It had been quite some time since my last visit however I had kept hearing a voice in my head telling me to go, so go I did!

That evening prior to the event starting the psychic medium was sitting in the front of the audience. As soon as I walked in she turned around and looked directly at me and continued to watch me until I took a seat with the rest of the audience. It's difficult to describe the feeling I had at that moment nonetheless I was 100% certain that she was going to come to me with a message.

When her session commenced she stood up in front of the audience and without a moment's hesitation she pointed directly at me. She informed me that she had a very strong presence of a male figure that was extremely persistent and insisted that she give me a message. After validating with her who this person was, with information only known to me, he told me that I was my own worst enemy and despite all the ideas I had there was only one thing holding me back and that was myself. He went on to add that I had already woken up to the journey that I should take, which was very true, and he went on to add that I just needed to have the confidence in myself to take that leap of faith.

He reassured me that he would be standing at my side from now on to give me that push that I needed. This message was from my father who had sadly passed away a couple of years earlier from pancreatic cancer and whilst we hadn't always seen eye to eye whilst he was alive, this communication with him had given me the motivation and support I needed.

These two events were what triggered my decision to commence writing this book, and from start to finish the whole process took me less than 6 months, which for me is no mean feat!!

The Psychic Nerd

As I began to make progress with my book I began to realize what a path of discovery for me it has been and how cathartic the whole experience has been. You can imagine as a young boy I grew up thinking that these strange things that were happening to me were somewhat strange but because they happened so often they just became a normal part of my life.

Don't get me wrong as a young child right up to adolescence I encountered situations that scared the hell out of me, however I have been fortunate enough to meet people along the way that have helped me to understand at least in part some of the happenings that I encountered and indeed continue to encounter to this very day.

From what I have been told by nearly all spiritual people I have chanced upon with similar skills over the years is that I subconsciously lock out my skills. I must admit this is quite true especially when I was younger. On the many occasions where I have had the best results it has been when I have opened myself totally to what is happening and it is my intention with the appropriate assistance and guidance I will be able to develop and expand my ability and use my gift in a positive manner.

I am a very private person and don't promote my skills to everyone, indeed there are many members of my extended family who to this day are not aware of these skills I have.

I recently went back to the United Kingdom on holiday, whilst there I finally discussed the subject with my mother to see if any family members had similar skills as they say it can be inherited. It was interesting to hear that my maternal grandmother had often attended a spiritualist church and had taken a keen interest in psychic mediums. My mother also hinted that there may have been other family members with psychic tendencies in the family though she would not elaborate further. Unfortunately I do not recall meeting my maternal grandmother as regrettably she died when I was only one year old; at least she got to meet me and I often wonder if I inherited my special gift from her, who knows?

Chapter 2

The Beginning – Mind Your Head

The Psychic Nerd

It was a dark stormy night, the moon was full and there was strong winds in the air……..hold on I said this was not going to be dramatized so let's start again!

I come from a working class family from Liverpool in England. I am the youngest of 5 siblings (4 boys and 1 girl) and was brought up by my Mum and Dad. We were just an average family of the time, growing up in Liverpool in the 70's and 80's my parents never really had much money. My Dad didn't work due to a medical condition and my Mum worked several cleaning jobs in order to make ends meet. Despite this, my parents still managed to put food on the table, clothes on our back and raise 5 fairly well adjusted young adults and for this I have total respect for the hard work and effort this required.

Before we continue, I would like to give a brief description of the house we lived in; it was a typical three bedroom semi-detached council house. Upstairs there were three bedrooms, a bathroom and a small landing area. Downstairs consisted of a long living room with a single door to the kitchen. In the kitchen there was an external door which led to a small outhouse or 'owdyhouse' as we used to pronounce it which leads to the front door. To get to the stairs you had to walk through the kitchen, through the outhouse room and then from the hall adjacent to the front door.

At this point in time I was approximately 8 years of age; it was just a regular Sunday afternoon with most members of the family going about their own business. Dad was in the kitchen cooking dinner with the other 6 members of the family congregated in the living room.

Suddenly we all heard a tremendous bang and seconds later my Dad came running into the living room, he was quite shaken up and was demanding to know who the hell had thrown a small gas canister at his head. Obviously, we had all jumped when we heard the noise and then to see my father running in the living room, with the canister in his hand had really unnerved us all, especially when my Father seen us all together in the room.

The gas canister in question was approximately the size of a deodorant can and my Dad had actually thought that one of us had been misbehaving in the outhouse room as the canister was usually positioned on top of a cupboard in that room, and it was from that direction that it had been thrown from. It had been thrown, quite a distance, with such force, that the canister had buckled in half and left an indentation on the door. My Dad had actually heard it flying at him and managed to avoid it hitting him. When he realized that none of us could be responsible for this act he went rather quiet, as indeed did the rest of the family as there was no reasonable explanation to account for what had just happened.

I can still to this day remember each one of us looking at the other and wondering how this object could have been thrown when we had all been in the living room together. In hindsight I think we were all rather shocked so were genuinely didn't know what to think.

Despite my young age I can vividly remember wondering how this could have been thrown at my father, the head of our family, and to see him quite shaken up was somewhat distressing. My parents could not explain to us what had happened and looking back I think initially they tried to play down what had happened that afternoon, little did we know at the time this was the 'hello' moment from our new tenant.

Chapter 3

Feeling a Presence

Over the next couple of weeks some really strange things started to happen at home. Items that had been left in one room would appear in a different room sometimes almost instantaneously, for example my Mum would leave her purse in the living room, walk upstairs to her bedroom and her purse would be on the bed despite having left it downstairs minutes earlier. As these incidents started to escalate family members, especially siblings, would accuse each other of moving the items. On a lot of occasions the items would disappear for weeks at a time and then appear in some really unexpected areas. Missing items would often include keys, letters, toys, clothing and money.

As a young child I became aware of these events gradually, I believe my parents tried to protect the youngest members of the family from what was going on.

My sister at this time would have been around 11 years of age and she had very long straight hair. One day I could hear my mother and sister talking in whispered tones, and being a rather inquisitive child I tried my best to hear what they were talking about.

From what I could ascertain my sister was explaining to my Mother that she felt like something was following her when she was walking up the stairs and on numerous occasions she had her hair pulled when no one was around her. My Mother tried to reassure her that there was nothing to worry about but these types of incidents continued to occur and we all began to feel as though we were being watched or followed around the house. It's a difficult feeling to try and explain but it was quite apparent that we were all being affected in one way or another.

Over time the family started to encounter noises from areas of the house that were unoccupied. For example if we were all in the living room together loud banging would start in the kitchen or upstairs from one of the bedrooms. Sometimes late at night when everyone were sleeping upstairs we would be woken by a loud noise coming from downstairs, despite the house being in darkness and everyone, until that point, fast asleep.

All these strange incidents were beginning to escalate however up until this point I had never encountered our new tenant on a one to one basis until this episode.

The Psychic Nerd

Despite sharing a bedroom with my 3 older brothers, in 2 sets of bunk beds, I had always been a very good sleeper but one night I was very restless and was constantly being awoken by the slightest movement or noise. I awoke up for some such reason in the early hours of the morning, and all I can remember hearing at the time was my brothers' deep breathing around me.

As I mentioned, the 4 of us shared the same room, we all slept in bunk beds and I used to sleep on the bottom bunk furthest from the bedroom door.

Whilst lying awake in my bed I was suddenly aware of noises coming from downstairs, I then heard footsteps walking on the kitchen floor, and then the footsteps continued into the outhouse. Whatever it was or whoever it was I knew they were at the bottom of the stairs, I then heard very slow steps come all the way up the stairs; I remember lying in bed with an overwhelming sense of foreboding, despite being such a young age I could sense that whatever was approaching had a malevolent presence. The footsteps continued slowly and then abruptly halted directly outside my bedroom door, a moment later the door handle turned and the door very slowly started to open. Despite knowing otherwise, I was hopeful that it was my Dad coming in to check on us. I tried to call out but was unable to get the words out. My three brothers were all still asleep and at this point I was hiding under the covers right over my head with just a little peephole to see and breathe through. Then the door opened a little further and a glowing light started to spread from the open door to the corner of the room directly by my end of the bed to the corner of the room. My heart at this point was pounding and within what felt like minutes but was probably only a few seconds, the door was slammed shut and still my brothers slept through it.

As I'm sure you can appreciate a million and one things were going through my mind at that stage, and I was so afraid that I hid under my covers all night until I eventually fell asleep but I was unable to leave my bed until I heard my brothers waking up in the morning. Once I was up I immediately found my Mum and Dad and asked if either of them had been up late in the night, despite knowing in my heart that they had not been. I went on to explain to them what I had experienced during the night and inevitably they tried to play it down and telling me I' had a bad dream, however despite my young age, even then I knew it was anything but.

Inexplicably these nightly visits continued for quite some time, always overwhelming me with a sense of foreboding and trepidation and I always felt that I was being solely targeted for reasons unknown. There would be times when I would literally try and shake my older brothers awake by kicking or poking their bunk beds from below, just to have the reassurance of hearing their voice would allow me sometimes to have a good night's sleep.

I continued to tell my parents of these events whenever they happened; my mum's advice was to come into their room to sleep which I gratefully welcomed. I would on numerous occasions be awoken by the sound of the sinister footsteps downstairs and before they would continue closer to me, I would seek solace by running to my parents' room and jump in their bed; sleeping between my parents would bring me instant relief and an overpowering feeling of security. On other occasions I would just lay in my bed unable to sleep with an impending feeling of menacing which would again lead me to beat a hasty retreat once again to my parents' bedroom. On these occasions an Olympic sprinter would have been unable to beat me running across the landing to my parents' room!

As I grew a little older I tried to remain in my own room with my brothers as often as possible however I continued to be awoken by the nightly visits which always resulted in me hiding under the covers as fast as possible. Despite numerous visitations they were never anything more than that, no direct communication ever.

At that time in my life these were the most frightening experiences I had ever encountered however looking back now older and wiser I realize this was just my initial introduction to what my spiritual future would hold.

Chapter 4

Seeking Solace in Religion

The Psychic Nerd

Our family worshiped at the local church which was Church of England (Protestant); my siblings and I all attended Sunday school from the age of 7 up to around the age of 12 and my parents attended church every Sunday. Our local church was located about 20 minutes away from our home.

Since our initial encounter with our house guest that hurled the gas canister at my Father, more than 3 years had passed and the strange happenings continued on a regular basis to all family members. As a family although we did not really ignore what was happening we strangely, for the most part, became accustomed to them. However it was an unspoken rule that we did not discuss these matters outside of our family.

This did not mean that family members did not discuss what was going on and on several occasions during such conversations I would hear the word 'poltergeist' being mentioned. At that time I had absolutely no idea what a "poltergeist" was and you couldn't exactly go and Google it in the early 1980's. The only avenues we had at the time to source such information was the local library.

I spent a lot of time at the library as I loved the peace and quiet and I would spend hours there drawing pictures from the illustrated books and it was on one such visit that I took the opportunity to learn more about what a poltergeist was. The definition of the word could not have summed up more accurately what had been happening in our home for the past 3 years.

Events became so frequent that we associated a name to the poltergeist and called him 'Charlie'. This may seem that we had a rather blasé attitude about the whole situation but realistically it was easier for us to try and make light of what was going on rather than to dwell on the negativity. By giving the poltergeist a name it seemed to enable us to blame 'Charlie' for anything untoward or unexplained that we had encountered.

One of 'Charlie's' favorite tricks was to play around with the house lights and other electrical objects. Occasionally my brother and I would be home alone for short periods of time. We would usually be watching TV together and when my parents arrived back home every single light and lamp would be switched on in every room in the house, radios would be quietly playing and the kettle would be switched on and boiling away.

Other activities included banging noises from rooms that were empty and also loud footsteps running up and down the stairs.

Despite these playful actions, 'Charlie's' exploits started to escalate and were starting to become somewhat more menacing and disturbing.

Not knowing where to turn to for guidance, my parents eventually plucked up the courage to approach our church for advice. After some questioning from the vicar he insinuated that these events could not be possible and we must have all been imagining it. I can only imagine how utterly hopeless and dejected my parents must have felt at this time. My parents pleaded with the church for their help but were steadfastly refused. The vicar told my parents that no formal body existed within the church to deal with this type of phenomenon, however, despite their continued refusal at this point in time, we cannot write off their support just yet, as will be revealed later in this book.

Before I continue any further, and totally unconnected to any of the events happening at that time at home, I just want to digress and give you some background on my grandparents.

My paternal grandparents were known to me as Nan and Granddad. Unfortunately, my maternal grandmother had passed away when I was aged just 1 however my maternal grandfather also known as Granddad lived until I was in my late 20's.

My Nan was the most amazing woman you could meet and she was the matriarch of our family. She was always happy to see us and ready to shower us all with lots and lots of love and affection. To say that I adored her would be an understatement and just to make her even more perfect in my eyes my Nan baked the most amazing delights. To this day the smell of freshly baked scones or homemade apple pie takes me back to the comfort and security of her home instantly. After my Nan had been baking I tell you I could have quite happily slept in her pantry!

Now as much as I loved my Nan and would have happily liked to have seen her 7 days a week if that had been possible, I was always very wary of the lady who lived next door to my Nan. This lady had never been malicious or unkind to me but I just had an overwhelming feeling of apprehension and uneasiness even just walking past her house. As is normal for me I'd never confided to anyone about my fears and once I reached the safety of being inside my Nan's home my fears were forgotten until it was time to leave.

For quite some time I had been having very vivid dreams about this lady. Every dream was the same and she would constantly chase me but I would always wake up before she ever caught me.

I confided to my siblings about these dreams and when they were somewhat dismissive of what I was telling them, as siblings can be, I went on to tell them that I had a theory about this lady but I couldn't tell them what my theory was for various reasons. Of course this announcement had ignited their curiosity, so after considerable persuasion I finally told my siblings that I thought this lady was a witch. Predictably this statement provoked much hilarity from them all. I then went on to add that now I had told them my opinion, something would happen to the lady; again this was met with laughter and looks of disbelief.

Imagine their shock and astonishment when the following day we received the news from my Nan that her neighbor had unexpectedly died in her sleep that night.

Was this a premonition of some kind or purely a coincidence? Who can say with 100% certainty? What I do know is that my opinion about this lady to this day has never wavered despite being older and wiser and if I ever drive past her old home it still sends a shiver down my spine.

Chapter 5

The Jester

The Psychic Nerd

My father had purchased a new camera, very high tech for its time and the type of camera that processed the image instantly and delivered a photograph within seconds from the base of the camera.

A few days after purchasing the camera, my father, my second to oldest brother and myself were all together in the living room. (The other 4 members of the family were out for the evening). After familiarizing himself with the camera for a few days there was just one film left to use so my father held up the camera and pointed it at a full length lampstand in the corner of the room, pressed the button to take the image and then waiting for the photograph to be processed and printed.

It took around 60 seconds for the picture to fully develop but when it did we could not believe our eyes, clearly visible in the picture was a tall figure with an arm held rather protectively over its face. This figure was in blue and red colors and was clearly dressed in clothing similar to that of a court jester type costume; you could even see the tassels and bells on the elbows and wrists. The picture clearly showed the alternating red and blue of the costume just like something out of a history book.

I can tell you this image sent shivers down our spines it was so clear. Could my father inadvertently have captured an image of the mischievous Charlie? I recall having a conversation with my father and brother about this photograph and whether in fact we had obtained an image of Charlie or perhaps something else. Whatever it was in that photograph it had been totally surprised, perhaps by the flash, or the fact it had been caught on camera.

I hinted at the possibility of the photograph disappearing, as regular objects often did and now that an image of Charlie may have been captured I was doubtful that this photograph would remain in our possession. My father assured me he would find a safe place in the house where he would keep the photograph out of harm's way.

Reluctantly I went to bed and when I woke the next morning I was eager to see the reaction of the rest of the family when they set eyes upon the photograph. My father went to retrieve it from his so called safe place, and yes it had disappeared.

Now I appreciate the skeptics amongst us will think that no such image ever existed however I can assure you that the three of us witnessed what was captured on that image and it was so clear that it shocked us all, probably more so than the disappearance of the photograph itself.

You could hide nothing from Charlie and we certainly learnt a valuable lesson that day.

Up until the day we moved out of that house, I often hoped that the picture would reappear as missing objects often did but the jester in the photograph obviously never wanted to return this piece of lost property to us.

Chapter 6

Asteroids

The Psychic Nerd

During the course of my childhood I encountered many alarming and worrisome experiences however what I am about to relate to you was by far one of the most frightening. I was approximately 12 or 13 years old at the time and late one afternoon I was home alone in the main living room of the house, in this room we had a 4 seat couch and two single chairs. I was sitting in one of the single chairs playing away on the Asteroids game on our new Atari console. This game console was connected to a small portable television and they were both situated on a trolley which was right in front of me.

I was happily playing for what seemed like hours and even happier that I had the games console all to myself for once!! I was somewhat absorbed in the game, playing well and reaching my highest score; then I lost all my lives and it was game over. Out of frustration I tossed the joystick towards the console and cursed myself for being beaten.

At that very moment one of the cushions on the couch opposite flew into the air and landed on the floor directly in front of me and instantaneously I could hear a loud, demonic laugh so vividly that the devil himself could have been standing next to me at that very moment. As soon as the laughter started and the cushion was sent into air, time appeared to just stand still and I couldn't move. I was frozen to the spot like a cartoon character and then the laughter boomed at me again and seemed to bring me to my senses. Within a split second I jumped out of my chair, ran to the cabinet where all keys were kept as all my senses were telling me to get out of the house. I frantically scrambled for the keys as I could sense a presence so close to me it was as though we were glued together.

Despite my panic I grabbed the keys and ran as fast as I could through the kitchen, through the outhouse straight to the front door. It seemed to take forever for me to reach the door, and when I finally opened it I literally fell head first onto the front garden. At almost the same time, two of my friends were walking past my house and I think they were quite startled to see me running out of my house in a somewhat distressed state. To say that I was happy to see them would be an understatement. At this point my heart was beating rapidly and the heat I could feel coursing through my body was overwhelming so it was more than obvious to them both that something had disturbed me. I had on previous occasions recounted to them about some of the happenings at our house so when I had finally composed myself I still didn't feel brave enough to return to the house, and of course neither of my friends would enter the house with me so we all sat together in the garden until my parents returned home.

From this point in time the disturbing events in the house started to intensify and were much more menacing and after much deliberation as a family, my parents had no alternative but to return to the church to seek help.

Eventually after much encouragement and persuasion from my parents, the powers that be from the church reluctantly agreed to send a representative to investigate; the person they were sending as far as we knew was to gauge, merit and record the events happening in our home.

Chapter 7

Now Get Out

The Psychic Nerd

I can remember the following events so vividly and whilst they were shocking from my prospective they were very thought provoking.

My brother, who was closest in age to me, was actually only 16 months older and most school days we both usually went home together for lunch as we lived relatively close to our school.

On one such day, we were both home having lunch when there was a knock on the door. My father answered the door and there was a man standing outside dressed in black with the telltale while collar showing and he was carrying a black briefcase/bag.

He introduced himself as being a representative from the Church of England and though somewhat taken aback by his unexpected visit, my father invited him into our home. Although I am not sure of his official title for purpose of reference I will refer to him as a vicar.

As soon as the vicar stepped foot in the hallway of our home he immediately placed his hand on his chest, his breathing became increasingly labored and he was struggling to catch his breath. After a couple of minutes he appeared to become more calm and described to my father that upon entering our house he had been overwhelmed by a coldness and a rather sinister presence and it had taken all of his strength to regain his poise.

My father led the vicar into the kitchen whereupon he instantly set his eyes upon my brother and me quietly sitting eating our lunch. After a somewhat whispered conversation between my father and the vicar it transpired that he was not merely paying a social visit but had in fact come to the house to make an assessment and if necessary to perform a cleansing. The word exorcism was never spoken however the vicar suggested to my father that it was not advisable for my brother and me to be present during his time at the house. Rightly or wrongly my father declined his request politely informing the vicar that compared to what our family had been living with over the past few years we were entitled to stay.

Reluctantly the vicar accepted my father's decision however he insisted that we stay in the kitchen whilst he accompanied my father around the rest of the house. Before he went upstairs he collected his black bag and took out a bible, a bottle of holy water and a purple colored stole which he draped around his neck. He then went upstairs holding his bible and holy water in one hand and with his other hand he once again started clutching his hand against his chest while taking large deep breaths. He then disappeared out of our view but we could still hear what was going on and believe me the volume was about to increase.

From downstairs my brother and me could hear the muffled conversation and the footsteps above us and then suddenly we heard a deafening pounding noise and we both thought the ceiling was going to come crashing down upon us, it really was that loud and the whole house seemed to shake. Every time the vicar moved to and from different rooms upstairs this booming noise followed him and it seemed to be getting louder on each occasion. We were cowering together downstairs, and perhaps regretting the earlier decision that our father had made on our behalf about us staying home, but at the same time too afraid to make a run for it for fear of the unknown. After what felt like an eternity but in reality was really only about 20 minutes the vicar, followed by my father, who unsurprisingly appeared somewhat ashen, started coming downstairs and as they did so an eerie silence descended around the house.

The vicar, now appearing a lot more assured and composed, continued his tour of the house downstairs and the silence continued; the thunderous bangs that we had been subjected to only minutes earlier had finished as abruptly as it had started.

After completion of his duties, the majority of which we had not been privy to, the vicar explained to my father he was confident that the future in our household would be far less traumatic and that he did not envisage us encountering any future similar problems.

For the most part he was correct, from that day forward we did not experience any objects disappearing or in fact being thrown at us, no unexplained noises, no hair pulling, no inexplicable footsteps, voices or visits in the night; it all just ceased and our home seemed like a different place without any threat or menace hanging over us. We did however have one final encounter some months later from a much loved source.

The Psychic Nerd

We had a few further visits from the church after this just to check our progress and during one such visit it was implied by the vicar that the reason for all the troubles we had lived with could have been due to our involvement with martial arts which they had deemed to have connections to the occult! My father was somewhat taken aback by such a ludicrous suggestion but apparently it had noted that we had been attending regular Judo classes and what was even more ironic was the fact that these classes were actually held in the church hall.

On reflection I truly think they were just clutching at straws with this suggestion regarding our attending martial arts. I'm sure they had no idea how this 'spirit' had arrived at our home, but I do believe the members from the church knew exactly what it was we were living with yet despite this our family's initial requests for help seemed to fall upon deaf ears. Thankfully they did come to our assistance in our hour of need but what took them so long? Even if they had just come to assess our circumstances in the first instance rather than steadfastly refusing our requests for help would have made a huge difference to our lives and what we were living with on a daily basis. Whilst it is not something the church makes public they do have sectors within their organization to deal with such matters so I wonder why they were so reluctant to help.

Thankfully as a family we were strong enough to get through all that we had endured but little did we know that we were about to suffer such a loss that would leave us all heartbroken.

I mentioned my Nan to you earlier; she truly was a special person and the matriarch who held our family together. We all adored her and she in turn loved us all unconditionally. She was such a big part of our life and then she was gone. My Nan passed away on Mother's Day and whilst her death was not unexpected the void that she left was never filled.

My Nan had been ill for some time and my parents seemed to be at the hospital visiting her whenever possible. On the day she died my parents had literally just arrived home only to receive a call advising them to return back to the hospital as her condition was deteriorating. I can remember sitting in my bedroom just knowing this was the day she was going to pass and if there was any consolation I knew she would at least be out of pain but when my parents returned home later that day to inform us that we had lost her I was still unprepared for the grief that I felt.

The days after her death passed in a blur with the usual plans being made for her funeral and gathering of family and friends offering condolences. At her funeral we gave her the sendoff that she deserved, and it was the first funeral I ever attended and though rather overwhelmed by the finality of it all I gained some comfort in being part of her final farewell.

Just a few days following her funeral one of my elder brothers woke up at about 1:00 am to go to the bathroom, the rest of the siblings were sleeping and my parents were still awake downstairs. As my brother left his bedroom to walk across the landing my Nan suddenly appeared in front of him just floating in the air. She did not verbally communicate with him but in his mind he received a message from her which told him "tell everyone I am happy where I am and not too worry". As soon as my Nan had given him this message she just disappeared in front of him, as quickly as she had appeared. My brother was 18 years of age at this time, and after this happened he ran downstairs to my parents in a very distressed state eventually explaining to them what he had just encountered.

The next morning my brother was still visibly upset by the incident the previous night and my parents explained to us what had happened. I recall not being alarmed by what they told us and if anything I was somewhat intrigued and perhaps a little jealous of my brother that he had one final meeting with my Nan however little did I know that years later my Nan would pay me a visit when I least expected it.

Following on from this our house was quiet and uneventful for more than 9 months until the morning of New Year's Day. My parents, my brothers and I were together in the living room and my sister was alone upstairs. As my sister walked down the stairs to join us we all heard a very loud whistling to the tune of Yankee Doodle Dandy. This whistling was loud, clear and didn't miss a beat and it followed my sister as she walked from the top to the bottom of the stairs. Every one of us in the living room heard the whistling but the strangest thing was that my sister did not hear a sound and was somewhat bemused to see us all staring at her as she entered the room. Now for anyone skeptical of this tale I can confirm that my sister could not whistle anything let alone a perfect rendition of Yankee Doodle Dandy!!

At this point we were all bewildered by what had just happened and someone uttered that Charlie was back much to everyone's alarm but thankfully after that incident nothing again ever happened in our house and peace and normality returned.

I personally like to think that at that point in time my Nan was around to protect and shield us from anything untoward and trust me when I tell you no-one would want to antagonize her when it involved her family!

Chapter 8

Growing Up

The Psychic Nerd

When I was around 16 we moved house and although it was still a 3 bedroom house the rooms were a lot bigger and so we all had a lot more room. This new home was a fresh start for the whole family, and it enabled us to put all the past happenings from our old house behind us; a brand new start.

I often thought about the family that had moved into our old house and wondered if they had every encountered any similar events to us however this I will never know but I always hoped that it had remained as peaceful as it was when we eventually moved out.

In the summer of 1983 I left school and made my first tentative steps into my career in the IT industry as a junior programmer; I remember whilst I was still at school discussing my future career options with my teacher and when advising her of my intentions she was somewhat surprised and tried to steer me into a different direction especially as IT was such a new industry at that time she felt it was a risky choice. Despite her negativity I would not be swayed in my decision and somehow knew that IT was what my future profession would be and thankfully I can report that I have carved out a most successful career in this field and continue to do so to this day.

During my years as a young adult I never had any concept that I was psychic, that all came later. I was however starting to experience frequent déjà vu events and my recollections were very detailed and accurate along with this I also seemed to have an uncanny ability in judging peoples' character and on the rare occasion when I did go against my initial instincts it was always to my detriment; with this in mind I have welcomed people into my life who I ordinarily may not have embraced and have remained lifelong friends.

At the age of 18 years I left my hometown of Liverpool and moved to Sheffield. Shortly after I left Liverpool, the health of my paternal Grandfather started to decline and he unfortunately ended up being housebound. During this time I returned to Liverpool as often as possible to visit him and as his health rapidly started to deteriorate we all took it in turns to stay overnight with him as it was his final wish to not be admitted to hospital for as long as possible. During one such evening when I was staying with him, we spent an incredible evening together one that I will never forget it. Despite his failing health and his fading memory we spent the entire evening talking about everything and nothing. He reminisced about different times throughout his life from being a young boy to right up to where he was at that point in time, and he inevitably knew that his time with us was sadly coming to an end. It was fascinating listening to his anecdotes of a bygone era and a memory I will always treasure.

The following day I was preparing to leave him to travel back to Sheffield and as I was saying goodbye to him, I said I would come back to see him the following weekend. He looked me directly in the eye and calmly explained to me that this would be the last time I would see him as he would be joining my Nan very soon. I gently hugged him and told him not to be silly and I would see him again soon. I said my goodbyes, he smiled and said goodbye.

A couple of days later back in Sheffield, I awoke in the middle of the night with an overwhelming feeling of despondency and the first thought that came to my mind was my Granddad. I tossed and turned for the rest of the night and cold think of nothing else but my Granddad. I eventually drifted back off to sleep and early the following morning awoke to the sound of the telephone ringing. Before I even took the call I instinctively knew that my Granddad had passed away, bizarrely almost at the moment that I had awoken in the early hours.

The sadness and guilt of not being with him when he passed hit me hard and then to further compound my grief I did not attend his funeral and remained in Sheffield a decision I will always regret. My reasons for not attending his funeral were due to family difficulties at the time which I unfortunately let cloud my judgment. Regretfully I made the wrong choice and obviously it was a mistake I could never rectify though I know my Granddad would have understood and forgiven me no matter what.

In time I moved back to Liverpool to live with my parents and one day we chatted about my Granddad and about his last few days they had spent with him. Seemingly on the night he passed away he was with my parents and also my Dad's two sisters, he was still at home, as he had requested and they were all seated around his bed.

The Psychic Nerd

My Granddad kept staring past them into the same spot in the corner of the room and smiling. This had happened quite a few times in a short period of time and my Aunt asked him what he was looking at, to which he calmly replied your Mum is here and she has come to take me with her. At this point in time, though near to death he was lucid and composed and those with him at that time accepted what he said probably in the hope that it brought him comfort.

Upon hearing this I can't say I was shocked by what he had said. It didn't surprise me that my Nan was waiting for him; I felt gratified to know that they had been reunited and he had not been alone as he made his transition.

I continued to live at home until I was 21 at which point I moved to Shropshire to take up a new position working with a well-known telecommunications company.

Initially I stayed in a local guest house and when I drove there for the very first time the house was very familiar to me. Even before I entered the house I correctly visualized many of the rooms inside right down to the very room that I would be assigned and I must admit I was somewhat unnerved when I realized how accurate I had been upon entering the house.

Despite such an unusual introduction to my new home, I lived there very happily with a delightful family for about 12 months. I then shared a house with a work colleague who was renting out a room. Once again when I first stepped foot into this house I had that same feeling of familiarity and recognized rooms and many features throughout the house. I have no idea why I felt so acquainted with both of these homes, in an area where until then I had never visited, but on both occasions I felt as though I was returning to a place that I had already been to, whatever it was if felt something more than déjà vu.

Despite living and working in Shropshire I had a girlfriend in Liverpool and I would return as often as possible to visit her and my family. On one such visit back home my girlfriend, my brother and I one evening called into our local pub for a drink. My girlfriend took a seat and myself and my brother went to the bar to order drinks. That night there was a new girl working behind the bar who was busy serving another customer but I noticed her immediately.

At that moment I discretely pointed her out to my brother and I said to him do you see that girl behind the bar serving drinks well I am going to marry her. This was 30 seconds after setting eyes upon her so you could appreciate that my brother was somewhat skeptical to hear me say this and not surprisingly he told me not to be so stupid, you don't even know her!! Undeterred by his response I resolutely replied that it didn't matter and that I would marry her.

Now obviously before I could marry this complete stranger I also had the issue of a current girlfriend to contend with!! Nevertheless once I have set my mind on something it is very difficult for anyone to change it. So as harsh as it may sound within a matter of days of making my decision, I ended my relationship with my current girlfriend and my next step was to become acquainted with the young lady who I hoped I would one day marry.

Obviously I was still working and living some 50 miles away from my "local" pub so it wasn't easy to just pop in for a drink. Fortunately for me at that time I worked shifts which resulted in my having 7 consecutive days off every month. During these days off I would spend my time in my local pub hoping that she would be working and if she was I had to sum up my courage in order to speak with her whenever possible. I had made some headway in finding out that her name was Helen but other than progress was slow!

As the weeks turned into months our relationship was little more than that of a polite acknowledgement for a regular customer so I decided to bite the bullet and ask Helen out on a date; a rather daunting undertaking in a busy bar knowing full well that this eye-catching young lady had already declined similar requests from other guys and yes you've guessed it my invitation was also declined on four separate occasions though Helen would maintain it was more like five or six attempts before she finally agreed to go out on a date with me.

Fortunately for me our first date was perfect, as were all our other dates thereafter and 16 months later I proposed whilst we were on holiday in Crete and I am happy to say Helen accepted my proposal. It was a very romantic proposal just as I had planned and a wonderful start to our future life together.

Our next step together was to buy our first home together. After months of searching the house we bought had a very unusual window design in the master bedroom and strange as it may sound I had already visualized this window many years before and somehow I knew this window be in our first home we bought together.

Over time I have now come to realize this is a recurring pattern and whenever we have subsequently moved house, there has always been something about our prospective new home that is very familiar to me and it is usually something a little unconventional. I now take it as a sign that I receive confirming that this is intended to be our new home and it is the right move for us. Thankfully it has worked for us so far.

After purchasing our first house and gradually making it into our new home, we married a few years later in the Caribbean with our closest family with us to share our special day.

We have now been very happily married for almost 20 years and have been together for 24 years so my persistence really did pay off and call it love at first sight, or something deeper than that, whatever it was I knew I was right to follow not only my heart but also my instincts and it positively worked for both of us.

Chapter 9

Heartbreaking Times

The Psychic Nerd

I have previously spoken about my bond with my paternal grandparents however my maternal grandmother passed away when I was very young and due to various issues and family fallouts our relationship with my maternal grandfather unfortunately was not so close and he was estranged from our family for many years.

Obviously as a child there was nothing I could do about this rift, and on the odd occasions when my Granddad Bob was reunited with our family I loved to spend time with him and listen to the stories that he regaled in telling us; so after my engagement to Helen I took it upon myself to reconnect with my granddad regardless of what the rest of my family thought.

So after a fair bit of research and a few false leads, Helen and I finally tracked him down living in a residential home approximately 30 miles outside of Liverpool.

Consequently a couple of days later I found myself anxiously outside of his residential home preparing to reacquaint myself with Granddad Bob.

Now before I go any further I need to give you a clear description of my Granddad; he was always very smartly dressed, a real gentlemen and very charming with the ladies. He had always maintained a high level fitness and in his earlier years had been a very keen boxer. Although he was of average height he had a rather stocky build and he cut quite an imposing figure.

So here I am waiting to meet my Granddad with some trepidation bearing in mind that I had not seen him since I was 12 years of age and not knowing what response I would receive from him when we did meet. I was now in my mid-twenties and standing over six feet tall so noticeably different since we had last met.

After confirming my identification with the staff at the residential home who I had informed in advance of my visit, I tentatively knocked on his door not knowing what to say or do when he answered.

He opened the door, looked at me from head to toe, a glimmer of recognition crossed his face then a smile and he put his arms up at me in a boxers pose. I did the same to him and we both just laughed. No words needed, all the lost years just melted away and it was a very special moment for us both.

When he first Helen he kissed her on her hand and turned to me with a twinkle in his eye and said if I was 20 years younger son you'd have a fight on your hands over this lovely lady!! I told you he was a charmer didn't I?

From that day forward we tried to meet up with him at least once a week. He absolutely adored Helen and the feeling was mutual he was the grandfather that she had never had and whenever we went out with him he would walk arm in arm with her and I didn't get a look in; to say I was a third wheel was an understatement but I loved it. I loved having my Granddad back in my life and I loved how he and Helen hit it off from the word go.

When we were out and about in the car, Granddad and Helen would sit together in the back of the car, whilst I chauffeured them around. On these occasions Granddad had a captive audience and enthralled us both with tales from his younger days. We all looked forward to spending these days together and I never regretted for a single minute my decision to track him down.

Regrettably a couple of years after we became reacquainted Granddad was diagnosed with cancer and his health deteriorated rapidly within a matter of months. We tried to make the most of what time he had left and spent as much time together as was possible, although his failing health prevented us from our usual days out we were just happy to sit companionably in his room and read to him, chat or just watch him sleep and ensure he was comfortable.

On one such visit I had gone alone as Helen had a cold and was mindful of transmitting germs to Granddad. I stayed with him for the best part of the day during which he had slept for the majority of the time. As I was preparing to leave he woke up and I explained to him that I would be back to see him in a few days and all being well I would bring Helen with me. He held his hand out to me and said you two always remember to do what is best for both of you, don't let anyone interfere in your relationship and always be the best of friends. I gave him a hug and left.

The Psychic Nerd

On my drive home I was in a rather reflective mood pondering over his words and how correct they were. I wondered if he was referring to my Mother with whom he had always had a rather difficult relationship with or was he just sharing with me the wisdom he had gained in his 80 plus years. Whatever it was he was alluding to I felt I had missed the chance to find out more about the reasons behind the family fall out and I had the distinct feeling that I would never have the opportunity to ask him about it.

The following day as Helen was feeling a little better we were debating whether it would be advisable to make an impromptu visit to see Granddad. For whatever reason I unexpectedly thought to myself that this discussion was futile and at almost the very moment this thought entered my head the telephone rang and then I had my answer Granddad had passed away and my heart felt as cold as the icy January day that it was. Helen and I hugged each other tightly, are grief engulfing us both and his words echoed in my ears - always be the best of friends, always be the best of friends.

Less than 2 months later we were at home getting ready to go to work when we received an early morning telephone call, you know the kind which 9 out of 10 times signals only bad news.

It was devastating news that we were totally unprepared for informing us that Helen's 18 year old nephew Steven, the son of her eldest sister, had died less than an hour earlier. I answered the call and at first couldn't comprehend this news and at this early stage details were still very unclear. I then had to break the news to Helen who was devastated as were the rest of her close-knit family.

We immediately left our home and drove directly to her sister's home where the rest of the family were congregating. Obviously everyone was in total shock and his sudden death at this time was still unexplained and a post mortem had to be performed. Both sides of the family stayed to support Helen's sister and her husband who understandably where devastated with the sudden and unexpected death of their son.

Now a couple of years earlier we had bought a boxer puppy who we named Tasha and although fully grown she still acted like a puppy and was very excitable, a typical boxer who was extremely affectionate and especially fond of Helen.

During this day I had returned home on a couple of occasions to attend to Tasha, feed her and take her for a walk, she was a real bundle of energy, very active and she was a much loved new addition to our family.

We both returned home in the early hours of the morning still stunned and shocked by what had happened. It was our intention to try and sleep for a few hours before returning to Helen's sister's home early the following morning.

Upon entering the house Helen and myself prepared ourselves for Tasha to come bounding towards us, as was her customary greeting however she was nowhere to be seen, which was most unusual. Helen went into the lounge and I went in search of Tasha only to find her still sitting in her bed on the landing upstairs. I managed to coax her downstairs, she tentatively walked into the lounge and suddenly stopped in her tracks when she noticed Helen. No matter how much Helen tried to persuade her to come to her Tasha would not budge. She stared intently looking past Helen, softly growling with all hairs on her neck standing on end. This continued for several minutes and eventually Helen stood up to comfort the dog but before she even got close to her Tasha bolted out of the room and stood cowering next to the door to the garden.

On top of everything that had happened that day, Helen was upset by the dog's behavior and I told her not to worry, to go to bed and I would take care of the dog.

No sooner had Helen left the room when the dog seemed to visibly relax and she sat on the floor next to me for a little while until I was ready to go to bed. I called her to the door to the garden to let her go outside and as I opened the door she froze on the spot staring into the darkness, growling and again all the hairs on her neck standing up.

Our garden was very private and secure and there was nothing there that could have agitated her but she would not step outside. Rather than forcing her I decided to let her just go to her bed on the landing which she did and the following morning her behavior had returned to her normal boisterous self and in the 10 or more years that she was with us after that night, she never behaved as she did that night, and I often wonder if Tasha had seen and sensed a lot more than what we were aware of.

Chapter 10

The Tutor

The Psychic Nerd

The next period of my life during my mid to late twenties is when I met a lady called Karen, who would open my eyes to a whole new world, a world of immense possibilities, oddities and new challenges and skills. Karen would become a very good friend and despite losing touch for several years, as the spirit world normally does, they find ways to reconnect people.

Karen did not know I was writing this book and for quite some time I had been trying to get back in touch with her, however for various reasons I had long since lost any contact details I had for Karen and I had exhausted all avenues of trying to contacting her again. Then quite unexpectedly and totally out of the blue several months after joining a business-oriented social networking service, Karen accepted an automated invitation that had been sent to all contacts from my Hotmail account, one such invitation had been delivered to an old email address that I incorrectly assumed she had long since abandoned.

Anyway back to the time about when Karen and I became acquainted, I had relocated to new offices in Warrington in the North West of England. After several months in my new role, I had heard from several colleagues that Karen was a psychic medium who also did tarot card readings and was always willing to give readings for her co-workers.

Now I have always had an interest in this area probably due to the events I had experienced whilst growing up, so one day I asked her if she would be willing to do a reading for me which she happily agreed to do so as soon as worked schedule would permit.

From my very first impression Karen was a very amicable, approachable lady and I was really looking forward to having a reading with her; I had never had one before and I was very intrigued by what it may reveal.

Weeks went by since my initial request and in the meantime a number of other co-workers had received readings from Karen. Initially I thought nothing of it but as time went by and I felt as though I had been overlooked, albeit perhaps unintentionally so one day I stopped Karen in the corridor and asked her when we could do my reading, she just looked at me and said we need to have a chat. I was rather shocked by her reply so we arranged to meet for coffee together that afternoon; I was rather curious to hear what she wanted to chat about.

We grabbed a coffee, sat down and immediately she told me not to be alarmed but she did not want to do my reading because she felt there were some serious forces at play that would not allow it. She was especially wary of doing the reading in a public place because she was not sure what would happen. She explained that the best way to describe how she was feeling about it would be similar to a Merlin-type character. Obviously I was rather confused by this analogy and wanted to know exactly what she meant so we arranged to meet in a private room in the building and ensured we were not disturbed.

We sat down across a small table and she then explained to me that forces around me were very powerful that were preventing any reading at all and the only way it would happen was if I was to give direct permission.

I gave my permission, she then put her tarot cards on the table and placed a Dictaphone next to the cards and started recording our conversation. Karen described with precise detail my childhood and many of the events that happened to me and my family. She confirmed my suspicions that the forces at play in my childhood home were directed at me and that this presence had been targeting me the whole time, a fact which I can tell you made the hairs on the back of my neck stand up. The accuracy of what she was telling me was unbelievable and it all started to piece together.

Karen told me that since our first meeting she was aware that the forces around me were extremely powerful and on a level equal to, if not greater than that of a psychic medium and in her opinion I had actually more ability than she did, I just did not know how to use it. This was a total eye opener for me; the vibes in the room were unbelievable, and when you have people with certain gifts together the energy generated can be very strong.

Following my initial shock and after taking several minutes out in order to compose myself, Karen then attempted to switch on the Dictaphone in order for us to continue where we had left off. After numerous attempts it would not work, it was as though the machine was being switched off and a somewhat exasperated Karen sat back in her chair and suddenly said to me can you please ask this gentleman beside me, who I believe is a family member of yours, to stop switching the Dictaphone off!!

She then proceeded to give a detailed description of this gentleman, who I immediately knew was Granddad Bob, her description was unmistakable and when she added that this man had only recently passed away it confirmed who it was to me 100%. Karen encouraged to me to speak to him so somewhat hesitantly I called out Granddad everything is OK please let us record the reading. The next time she pressed the record button and it worked perfectly first time.

As we continued Karen explained to me that I had lived many past lives as far back as Viking times and beyond; and that I had lived an assortment of lives over thousands of years always retaining my psychic skills. She added that this was the most prolific past life reading she had ever seen.

Karen then laid out her tarot cards on the table, at her request I selected fifteen cards with my left hand and placed them face down. She then started turning over the cards giving me feedback on each card once again with such accuracy it amazed me. The descriptions she gave about my childhood, my family and general things about my life were spot on. I was totally in awe of her skills and as you can imagine I wanted a reading; I did have a reading with bells and whistles attached.

She then gathered the cards and handed them over to me telling me it was my turn next to read the cards for her, I was a little taken aback at this request as prior to this reading I had never even seen a tarot card let alone have any knowledge of reading them.

I accepted the cards with some apprehension, shuffled them and gave them to Karen for her to make her selection. I then placed the 15 cards face down and began to turn them over one at a time.

Upon turning over the first card my mind was a total bank and I just looked at the picture on the card. Karen reassured me and told me to just try and relax, take my time and interpret whatever came into my head. I took a deep breath and continued turning the remaining 14 cards over, and whilst doing so I began to give an account of what I felt the cards represented to me. Karen was

The Psychic Nerd

very encouraging, informing me how accurate my feedback was of her and her life to this point. I was totally amazed and how well I had performed and afterwards I felt as though I had just past my entry examination into the psychic world.

The door was now open….

Chapter 11

Learning the Ropes

The Psychic Nerd

Upon discovering my new found skills I was very eager to learn how to develop and enhance these skills. Karen told me about groups of people who she knew with similar abilities to her who would regularly meet up in what they called circles; these circles involved likeminded people meeting on a regular basis to nurture their abilities and also make contact with the spirit world. It all sounded very intriguing and I was delighted when Karen invited me to attend one of the meetings and in particular meet one of the members called Michelle who was very highly regarded and was in fact a mentor to Karen.

Prior to the meeting I was both nervous and enthusiastic too but upon meeting Michelle all my nerves disappeared; I had an overwhelming sense of calmness which seemed to be exude from both Karen and Michelle especially when they were together. They both reassured me that even though I would be facing many new experiences I would always be safe.

The rest of the circle joined us and we sat around a large table in the kitchen of Michelle's house. I sat at the top with Michelle and Karen on either side of me. The meeting started with all the members of the circle giving projections of white light to protect and we all then said The Lord's Prayer together as a group both done as forms of protection.

We placed our hands flat on the table surface and Michelle then verbally invited spirits to come forward.

For what seemed like a long time nothing initially happened and as I mentioned earlier all of our hands were flat on the table, then very slowly my fingers on my right hand started raising from left to right tapping the table, it felt as if my fingers were playing keys on a piano and I had absolutely no control over it. I whispered to both Michelle and Karen that I was not moving my fingers voluntarily, it was happening and I was unable to stop it.

Both Karen and Michelle independently confirmed they had seen a lady's hand hovering above my hand before "floating" into my own hand. As they told me this I can tell you I was trying to remain composed but truthfully hearing this did freak me out and before I knew it suddenly my left hand started doing exactly the same and both hands appeared to be playing the piano in total unison and I had no idea what it symbolized.

Now at this point my whole body felt as though it was being pushed from behind and an intensive heat surged through my body especially around my neck and shoulders. Karen confirmed to me afterwards that she had never seen so many spirits come forward at any one time and they were all giving her the same message that they had been waiting for a long time for me to come and do this. Apparently the spirits were all behind me which would explain the surge of heat that I felt.

Karen also believed that the piano playing hands that she had witnessed was an indication that I had healing skills. She performed a test whereby I placed my hand over the top of her wrists to see how much heat I could generate. Apparently I generated so much heat that Karen was unable to leave her hands beneath mine for more than a few seconds.

During the evening I received several messages from members of my family who had passed over and I received an incredibly accurate message of validation from Helen's nephew.

So all in all my initiation into the circle had been quite an eventful one which had left me eager to know more.

Chapter 12

Life Changing

The Psychic Nerd

The next period in my life was not only when I turned 30 but, much more importantly, our family became three with the arrival of our beautiful son Lucas. I always knew Helen was going to give birth to a boy long before she was even pregnant.

Incidentally I have had considerable success in predicting the sex of babies before they were born. On one occasion I was at a social event with a group of friends and began talking to a couple who had only recently become romantically involved together. I had met the female on a couple of occasions before as we had a few mutual friends in common but I had never met her new partner.

After chatting for a little while to them both I informed them they would marry and have two boys in a very short period of time; which at the time I think they both just took with a pinch of salt. Several years later I bumped into them both, with their 2 little boys, yes she had given birth to 2 boys in very close succession, and they had married. She then confided in me that she always remembered our conversation from that evening mainly due to the fact that they had both been very skeptical in what I had told them largely due to the fact that for several years she had been experiencing gynecological/fertility issues and had resigned herself to the fact that she would probably never have children so I was even happier to know that my prediction had come true.

When Lucas arrived, some 18 days later than we were expecting, our lives changed for the better. He arrived at 1.47 am and I can remember shortly afterwards looking into the dark sky outside the hospital and thinking to myself that not only did I have Helen to take care of but now Lucas was the number one priority in both of our lives. As I'm sure all new parents can testify it was extraordinary for me when I held our beautiful new baby boy in my arms for the first time giving me an instantaneous bond which I knew would last a lifetime and far beyond.

As I mentioned earlier we had a family pet called Tasha who was a large, rather over protective boxer dog who for the first 5 years of her life had received our undivided attention and we were both a little apprehensive as to how she would react when she was introduced to Lucas.

Thankfully our concerns were totally unfounded, Tasha instinctively knew that this little person was now a new member of our family and from their very first introduction; she protectively placed herself on sentry duty close by to wherever Lucas happened to be and protected him from that point forward to her final days.

Chapter 13

Shadow Visitors

This story has always been very easy for me to recollect as it happened just a couple of days prior to the terrorist attack on the twin towers in New York on 9/11. This is a short story but very interesting.

During this period I worked from home on a full-time basis as an I.T. consultant. Our home was a double fronted detached property and my study was located on the right side of the house as you entered through the front door and to the left side there was a lounge, dining room, kitchen and conservatory. It was a very bright, airy house.

On the day in question I was taking a lunch break and was sitting in the lounge on a large couch which was close to the kitchen door, across the room to my right was an armchair next to the fireplace and to my left another armchair close to a window.

I was sitting watching the daily news on television when I suddenly caught sight of something in my peripheral vision and as I turned to see what it was four dark shadows in the shape of people were walking from the kitchen into the lounge. These shadows were so clear they looked like mannequins. They walked in single file into the lounge then two of the shadows sat next to me on the couch and the other two sat in the armchairs.

Simultaneously they all turned their heads and looked directly at me. I can remember vividly the shapes of the shadows were so clear you could actually see the legs bending as they sat down.

Now trust me at this point you would think I would jump off the couch and run for my life and to be truthful at the time that thought did not even enter my mind. I just sat and stared at them for what felt like minutes but was probably more like seconds and they just then stared back.

I then said out loud to them 'oh hello, what can I do for all of you'; as soon as I spoke they all just instantly disappeared before my very eyes. They didn't communicate with me in anyway and at the time I was more bewildered by what had happened than afraid.

I didn't think it was a sign of any sort although what happened just a few days later often made me wonder if perhaps it had been a sign or a warning of some description though this I will never know.

Chapter 14

Leave Him Alone

The Psychic Nerd

This episode in our life was one of the most trying and testing times for both myself and Helen. It was very disturbing as it involved Lucas, now aged 5, and I didn't know where to turn for help.

One Saturday evening all 4 of us were at home; Lucas had been asleep upstairs for a couple of hours whilst Helen and I were downstairs watching a movie and our boxer dog Tasha was snoring in front of the fire. Just a regular evening in the Daniels household.

Almost from day 1 Lucas has always been a very good sleeper and once he was in bed he regularly slept soundly for 10-12 hours but that evening at approximately 10.30 pm we both were alarmed to hear Lucas screaming from his bedroom, in a nanosecond I jumped up and raced upstairs with Helen not far behind me.

To be honest as I was rushing upstairs I thought he had either fallen out of bed (he had recently moved into a new cabin bunk bed) or he had experienced a nightmare. When I entered his bedroom, above his bed he had a trio of lights in the style of traffic lights and he used to sleep with a different light, red, amber or green switched on, so I could see him immediately still in his bed and still screaming. I climbed up the ladder, put my arms around him trying to comfort him assuming he had indeed had a bad dream.

However he was inconsolable, he wouldn't stop crying no matter how much we tried to reassure him. Between his sobs he was telling us that someone had been in his bedroom so in order to allay his fears and perhaps my own, I checked all the rooms upstairs and everything was in order.

After quite some time Lucas began to calm down and was lying in his bed with his Mum and he eventually drifted back off to sleep. We both crept out of his room, went back downstairs and thought nothing of it other than he had had a bad nightmare.

How wrong we were and less than an hour later it happened again only this time he was shaking, screaming and almost jumped off the ladder into my arms as I entered his bedroom. He was desperate to leave his bedroom, we took him downstairs and once again done everything we could to reassure him. He finally cried himself to sleep downstairs on the couch, we stayed with him and at about 1 am I carried him upstairs to his room as we were all going to bed at that time.

As soon as I stepped into his room I could feel his whole body tense up, he woke up immediately and started crying and saying please Daddy I don't want to go in there. What could I do? Helen took him from me and tried to coax him into his bedroom only to be met with the same response, to the point that he was becoming hysterical.

It was troubling for us both to see him like this especially as it was so out of character for him to behave in this way. Rather than distressing him any further we let him sleep in our bed for the remainder of the night hoping that whatever was disturbing him would be forgotten after a good sleep.

When Lucas awoke the next morning he didn't mention the events of the night before and rather than draw unwanted attention to it, we didn't mention it to him either. We spent the Sunday together with Helen's parents, as we often did as Lucas has always been very close to his maternal grandparents and after a hectic day out we returned home with a truly worn out Lucas, all ready for a good night's sleep ready for a busy day at school the following day.

All the usual bedtime preparations went as normal and as soon as I kissed him goodnight and Helen was taking him up the stairs he immediately started to get upset. He tightly held onto Helen's hand and told her that he didn't want to sleep in his bedroom and that there were people in his room. Again Helen tried to comfort him, telling him his room was safe and that no one was in there. We tried to persuade him into his room but he quickly became agitated, shaking, sobbing and with a raging temperature.

Once again it was very disturbing to see him obviously so upset and we couldn't explain why he was behaving this way.

This continued for the rest of the week, he was fine all day and absolutely inconsolable and distressed when it was time for bed. We met with his teacher who confirmed he had no issues at school and every other aspect of his life was trouble free. We thought of may have been suffering from night terrors however he appeared to be able to sleep peacefully anywhere other than his own bedroom. In the space of a week we had reached the stage that Lucas was now sleeping on a pull out bed in our room as failing that we would have been sleep deprived for the best part of 7 days.

Helen's parents stepped in to offer us some support and respite. They have always had a very close relationship with Lucas who absolutely adored both of them. We agreed for them to come stay with us for the weekend, hoping that their presence would help alleviate his fears and maybe if we left the house for the evening his usual bedtime routine might return with Nan and Granddad present.

After a little gentle persuasion Helen and I agreed to go out for dinner together and let the grandparents take charge.

Helen is the youngest of 5 children and her parents are very laid back and pretty unflappable and Lucas had been regularly looked after by both them from a very young age, all 3 of them were always happy to be together.

We were pretty disheartened therefore when later that evening we received a phone call from

Helen's Mum explaining to us that despite them both trying to get Lucas to bed for over 2 hours he was becoming increasingly distraught and they were both concerned about him. Obviously we returned home immediately to find a distressed little boy and two very anxious grandparents which only compounded our concerns.

Despite all our efforts the situation appeared to be going from bad to worse Lucas was becoming very inhibited, anxious and unsettled, he was now even refusing to play in his bedroom during the day and understandably the situation was affecting us all profoundly the longer it went on.

We sought help from our family doctor, spoke again to his school teacher and gratefully received any offers of help and advice from family and friends, all to no avail.

After we had been living with this situation for almost a month somewhat reluctantly I decided to take matters into my own hands in order to see if I could discover anything untoward.

The only reason for my reluctance was due to what I had lived through during my childhood and it was not something I wished for my son so I had tried to banish this theory from almost day one however it could no longer be ignored.

One evening after we had finally settled Lucas off to sleep, still in our bedroom, I then quietly walked into his bedroom and just sat on the floor, leaning against the wall. I switched on my radar so to speak and sat in complete darkness waiting to see if I could pick up on anything passing through or present within our home and in particular in my son's bedroom. After numerous attempts I had drawn a blank, I had not detected a thing.

The following day I approached my psychic friend Karen and explained to her what was happening, after listening intently to my recollection of events she then confirmed my fears.

Karen's opinion was that Lucas had inherited some of my skills and the people he kept saying were in his bedroom were spirits who were pushing too close to him whilst he was sleeping which was then waking him and understandably causing him to become distressed.

Karen did not feel that these spirits had any sinister intent and perhaps Lucas was just becoming a little more psychically aware, as some children often do.

She then advised me of what steps to take in order to rectify the situation and I left with mixed feelings as although I was hopeful of doing this I was perplexed by the news that Lucas may also be psychic, for reasons I stated earlier.

The following day Helen was at work and Lucas was at school which gave me the perfect opportunity to carry out Karen's instructions without being disturbed and more importantly without alarming my family, although Helen was aware of what I was intending to do.

Firstly I started in Lucas' bedroom, I stood in the centre of his room and confidently bellowed out 'whoever is within this house and keeps visiting my son Lucas I want you to know you are distressing him and it must stop immediately. If you do not comply with my request I will have no alternative but to make you stop and that's a promise'!!

I then repeated this request throughout every room in the house during which time the house was eerily quiet, there were no thunderclaps, booming noises or any signs whatsoever from my targeted audience and I was somewhat skeptical as to the efficacy of what I had carried out.

Several hours later Helen and Lucas arrived home together from school and we had our usual after school preamble which usually included milk and a snack for Lucas and coffee and a catch up on our day with Helen and myself. As Helen and I were chatting I suddenly became aware Lucas was no longer with us in the kitchen and assumed he was in the lounge playing with toys or watching television but he was nowhere to be seen. I checked the other rooms downstairs and again he wasn't there so you can imagine our surprise when we found him playing with his beloved garage and cars in his bedroom.

Helen and I exchanged glances and a feeling of relief swept over me, surely I couldn't expect such a successful result so quickly? We left him happily playing, daring to hope that we had finally turned a corner.

Bedtime came around that evening and rather than forcing the issue we had agreed that Lucas could remain sleeping in our room for the next few nights and we would hopefully try and ease him back gently to his own room if he continued to feel more comfortable in his bedroom.

That evening it was Helen's turn to take him to bed and as they approached our bedroom Lucas hesitated, turned towards his own bedroom and said I think I'll sleep in here tonight Mummy. Helen couldn't believe what she was hearing, she calmly led him into his room, watched him climb up his ladder, switch one of his traffic lights on and then get into bed.

Helen kissed him goodnight, left his door slightly ajar and practically skipped down the stairs to tell me what had just happened. I too couldn't quite believe what she was telling me, after all the upset we had endured over the past month surely we couldn't hope that it was over?

For the rest of the evening we both sat downstairs on tenterhooks waiting for Lucas to cry out to us, we didn't hear a sound. We then both went to bed, not before creeping into his bedroom to check on Lucas who was fast asleep, and that night I think we both slept with one eye open but thankfully Lucas slept right through and from that night forward he never had any further problems or disturbances with his sleep and everything returned to normality almost overnight it was a better result that we ever expected.

For several weeks afterwards we were very fearful that Lucas would have a setback but happily that never happened. I was so grateful to Karen and the guidance that she had given me and when I reported to her our positive news she assured me that we would have no further issues and I am happy to confirm that she was 100% correct.

Chapter 15

The Hangers

The Psychic Nerd

With the demands and responsibilities that come with parenthood my psychic development for the most part were put on hold when Lucas was a young boy.

We were very fortunate to have wonderful family holidays in some beautiful exotic places as far afield as Australia, America and The Caribbean and equally we were happy to spend quality family time together in a campsite in the UK.

One such holiday we spent time in a picturesque little coastal town in North Wales and we stayed in a holiday village that contained about 6-8 chalet type cottages and also in this holiday village was a very old farmhouse and barn which had been converted into a bar and restaurant.

Lucas was aged 7 when we went on this holiday and good friends of ours Jane and Simon joined us along with their 3 children.

Both families had cottages adjacent to each other and although not huge, the accommodation was clean, tiny with all the amenities required. The cottage comprised of a kitchen, a living area, 2 bedrooms and a bathroom.

One evening after both families had enjoyed a hectic day at the beach, Simon and I decided to go across to the bar for a beer before returning to cook a barbeque for everyone.

We walked into the bar, which was relatively empty, ordered our drinks and sat at a table close to the bar.

I looked to the very top corner of the restaurant area and could clearly see an old lady sitting in the top corner who was staring intently at me, even when I met with her gaze she didn't look away and for whatever reason she made me feel rather uncomfortable.

Simon was sitting with his back to this lady and after several minutes I actually said to him have you seen the old lady sitting in the corner, there is something not quite right about her. As he turned around and I looked again she had totally disappeared, I can tell you it sent a shiver down my spine.

Simon looked at me with a puzzled expression on his face and I assured him that moments earlier she had been sitting staring over to where we were both seated now it seemed that she had quite literally disappeared before our very eyes as her only exit out of the restaurant was just one door located behind us and no one had been in or out of it during the time we had been there.

We finished our beer and returned to our adjoining cottages and told Helen and Jane what had happened; they just laughed at us saying it was a good job we had only had 1 beer.

However what would happen later that night would certainly give me something to think about.

Following dinner the children were all exhausted after such a busy day and Lucas went to sleep in the front bedroom and several hours later we went to sleep in the bedroom at the rear of the cottage.

At approximately 1 am Helen woke me up as she was getting back into bed, I asked her if she was ok, she said everything was ok she had just been to check on Lucas. Now since he was a very tiny baby Lucas had always been a sound sleeper, very rarely awoke in the night and usually slept solidly for 12 hours so for either of us to get up in the night was very unusual. Helen told me all was ok and we both went back to sleep.

A couple of hours passed when I was woken by a faint, noise which was a continuous noise and it appeared to be coming from the direction of the room my son was sleeping in. It was now my turn to go and check on Lucas and to try and discover where the noise was coming from. Lucas was fast asleep and as I walked into his room the intensity of the noise increased and it was obvious it was coming from the wardrobe.

When I opened the wardrobe door the metal clothes hangers were moving, clashing together causing the sound that had awoken me.

They were swinging together as if someone or something was pushing against them. Initially I thought we had inadvertently left a window open or perhaps there was a draft coming into the room causing this to happen.

I had a quick check around and all the windows were closed, there was no noticeable draft and I went outside; it was very calm, not even a breeze but I could still hear the hangers clashing together. I tried to alleviate my uneasiness as sometimes I can be over protective especially when my family is involved. I checked again on Lucas who was still sleeping soundly blissfully unaware of how I was feeling. I again opened the wardrobe door and separated all the hangers.

As I was getting back into bed Helen was instantly awake and she suddenly said to me something doesn't feel right go and get Lucas. Upon hearing this from my very levelheaded, sensible wife, compounded with my own misgivings, I quite literally jumped out of the bed, ran into the other bedroom and grabbed a rather startled Lucas out of bed and handed him to Helen.

I ran back into the bedroom and all the hangers were bunched together again in the wardrobe, not swinging and not a sound had been heard by either one of us.

Lucas and Helen for the rest of the night slept in our bedroom and I sat up all night on sentry duty protecting my family. The following morning Helen told me when she initially woke that night at 1 am, she was overwhelmed with a sense of foreboding and her first instinct was to go check on Lucas. This was quite a surprise for me to hear this as Helen is very levelheaded and can on occasions be rather skeptical to paranormal phenomena.

For the rest of the holiday Lucas stayed in our room after some reconfiguration of the bedroom furniture and thankfully we had no further activities for the rest our stay there. We didn't experience any unease or disquiet that both had that night and went on to make happy memories of a wonderful family holiday with great friends.

At the time we were both mindful of the fact that what happened that night could well have triggered off a chain of events similar to what we had experienced in the previous chapter, but thankfully this didn't happen.

My own take on what happened that evening is that it was associated with the old lady who I had seen earlier in the bar area. I am convinced that she was paying me a visit to acknowledge that I had seen her and was making her presence known to me, albeit in a somewhat unusual way.

Chapter 16

Rachel's Friend

The Psychic Nerd

As I mentioned earlier in this book, even to this day there are members of my family who are not aware of the skills I have. One such family member was my sister-in-law Rachel who lived in Oxfordshire with her husband and son.

At this time I was working as an Oracle DBA and developer and was scheduled to attend a training course for 2 weeks in PL/SQL programming in a place called Cirencester which wasn't too far away from where my in-laws lived and they kindly agreed to put me up for the duration of my training course.

At that time, my brother-in-law Tom (Helen's brother) was away on a long tour of duty overseas with the Royal Air Force so when I arrived Rachel invited me to attend a night out with her and some colleagues from her workplace one evening later in the week. After what I knew would be a grueling week of studying ahead of me, I welcomed the opportunity of a break and readily accepted the invitation. A couple of days later Rachel and I were chatting about our imminent night out and the subject turned to a lady called Lisa who would be attending; she was a colleague of Rachel's and she was known for telling people their future and giving tarot card readings.

Upon hearing this my interest was immediately drawn to hear more about Lisa who apparently was a psychic medium who would often surprise people with spontaneous readings and from what I could determine she was very accurate in her predictions.

The following day I started to wonder if I met with Lisa later in the week it could possibly result in an awkward situation particularly for Rachel. When spiritual people meet for the first time they often recognize people of similar skills. If I enter a room I can quickly home in on anyone present with similar abilities. It's really strange and difficult to explain but I feel as though I am drawn to them like a magnet and on occasions I can see shadows or lights around them.

So getting back to a possible meeting with Lisa I was rather concerned that she too may sense my abilities which could lead to an awkward situation for my sister-in-law Rachel. After a discussion with Helen we both agreed it would be prudent to tell Rachel just in case this did happen.

The following evening I sat down with Rachel and as succinctly as possible tried to give her an overview of the real me. She was rather shocked by my revelation and promptly told me that she always knew there was something different about me but she wasn't sure what. We spent the rest of the evening discussing many of the tales I have recounted in this book and of course Rachel had an assortment of questions to ask me all of which I answered as honestly as possible.

The following night Rachel and I met with her colleagues in a local bar. As soon as we walked in I spotted a lady across the other side of the bar and even before we were introduced I instinctively knew it was Lisa. At the same time she suddenly looked across to us and came running up to Rachel and myself; she gave Rachel a welcoming hug and we were then introduced.

As soon as I shook her hand it was as though I'd just had an electric shock, she then fixed her gaze directly at me and said to me you've got it haven't you? Not wanting to give too much away I asked her what she meant to which she calmly replied, I know you have the same gift as me. Before I had an opportunity to respond further Rachel excitedly shouted out to Lisa oh my god he told me last night you would know he was psychic!!

Lisa and I spent the majority of the night swapping stories and being surprised at how many similarities in our experiences we shared. It was good to be able to talk to someone who could see matters from the same perspective as myself and it was a shame that the night ended so quickly.

Chapter 17

Cirencester Hotel Visitor

The Psychic Nerd

Several months later I was once again back in Cirencester for yet another I.T. training course. However this course was for just a week and I knew in advance it would be very intensive and would involve long days and late nights of studying so on this occasion I opted to stay in a local hotel close by to the training center.

For those of you who don't know, Cirencester is a market town in England, approximately 90 miles from London and is the largest town in the Cotswold District. Its history dates as far back as the Roman period and indeed it was the second largest town in Britain during Roman times so it has a long and esteemed history. The main street in the center of Cirencester is lined with historic buildings, some from as early as the Tudor era. The Fleece Hotel was one such building and was where I was staying whilst in Cirencester.

The hotel was beautiful, very historic and the room I had been appointed was very spacious, stylish and situated on the first floor directly above the hotel reception.

The first night I spent in the hotel I awoke startled, in the early hours of the morning and found myself sitting bolt upright in the bed. Despite the darkness of the bedroom I had a very strong feeling that someone was staring at me.

I switched on the lamp, there was nothing to see but I could still sense something, it really unnerved me, which doesn't happen very often. It took me at least an hour before I eventually went back to sleep and even then my sleep was very restless.

The following morning I woke up feeling exhausted due to such a bad sleep and not particularly in the best frame of mind for an intensive day of tuition ahead.

The next night I slept like a baby and I thought perhaps what I had experienced the previous night had been a one-off however the following night and all subsequent nights for the remainder of my stay I was awoken by the same feeling that someone was staring at despite the fact that it happened when I was fast asleep and the room was in total darkness.

On my final night staying in the hotel, after dinner I returned to my room to pack as much of my belongings ready for an early morning check out. I left out my clothes and toiletries for the next day and also some documents and coursework I was revising with that evening in preparation for my exam the next day

After spending several hours studying I went to bed and due to the impending exam I had I was desperate for a decent night's sleep so more thinking out aloud than anything else I said I know someone has been visiting me but try not to disturb tonight as I've an important day ahead tomorrow, or words to that effect. Unfortunately my request wasn't answered and once again I was awoken in the night, exact same scenario as previously, and out of sheer frustration I said whoever you are, I know you are here and you know I can feel your presence even if I can't see you!!

I tossed and turned for the rest of the night and it was morning before I knew it. I climbed out of bed and was amazed to see all my unpacked belongings strategically placed next to my suitcase. These items included my toiletries moved from the bathroom, my study notes moved from by bedside table and my laptop case which had been on the other side of the room, my clothes for that day remained untouched in the wardrobe but everything else was next to my suitcase. I was totally shocked. I took it as means of a validation or perhaps an apology for being disturbed all week, whatever it was confirmed my suspicions that I had indeed have an uninvited guest staying with me that week.

Chapter 18

The Dancing Bar

The Psychic Nerd

My psychic friend and mentor Karen often told me that I subconsciously locked out my abilities which I must admit I have to agree with her. If you can imagine someone telling you that you had these capabilities I'm sure you too would initially find it difficult to acknowledge or accept them. From my own personal perspective I really struggled; it was difficult for me to comprehend especially when I have such a logical thought process in relation to working within the IT industry so whether it was a subconscious decision or not I discovered that the most frequent occasions when I was contacted was when I had let my guard down and feeling relaxed and this sometimes happened when I had had a couple of alcoholic drinks.

On one such occasion I met my best friend David in the city after work one Friday afternoon for a couple of drinks. Pretty much the first busy bar we came across we went into and happily sat in a fairly quiet corner having a catch up. As most of the city workers filtered off home there weren't many of us left in the bar when suddenly a young lady stood in front of us in a very skimpy outfit asking us if she could dance for us, to say we were surprised was an understatement, we politely declined and it suddenly dawned on us what time of establishment this place was after dark – a lap dancing bar!!

We ordered a drink from her and at that very instant a male figure appeared to me and it was standing closely next to her. Immediately I knew that whoever this man was he had appeared in order for me to give this young lady a message.

I initially hesitated before I spoke to the lady whose name I later found out was Angie, as trust me when I say it's not always an icebreaker telling complete strangers you have a message from a loved one who has passed away some people don't take too kindly to such an approach. When Angie returned with our drinks the figure was still standing close by so casting aside any uncertainty I did have, I said to her now what I'm going to ask you may seem a little strange but if I describe someone to you, if you know who it is can you tell me; as expected she gave me a strange look and eventually nodded her agreement.

I started to describe the man who was standing clearly before me giving a description of his approximate age, height, build and then I mentioned a tattoo that was clearly visible on his right arm. As soon as I spoke about the tattoo she visibly trembled and sat down next to me. She was genuinely upset but she managed to tell me that the person I was describing was her older brother who had passed away a couple of years earlier.

She was very concerned about what he thought regarding the current job she was doing and I knew from her brother that he wasn't being judgmental or disapproving and I reassured her of this.

We then discussed details about her brother's passing, information about their childhood and although I didn't give her the full name of her brother I was able to correctly tell her that his initials were L.E.

With all this evidence validated by Angie sometimes with shrieks of incredulity we had managed to attract a small audience of about 4 or 5 of the other hostesses from the bar who were all asking me to tell them about loved ones they had lost or predict their futures. An assortment of questions and requests were being fired at me and in addition to speaking with Angie and her brother

I couldn't take much of it in, the only question I remember being asked was by a couple of the hostesses who both pointed to a lady who was serving behind the bar, and both asked me to tell them something about her. I stared at this lady for a couple of seconds and was told she had a boyfriend whose name was Nick. When I told them this they all started screaming and confirming that I was indeed correct and she had only met him three weeks earlier.

While all this was going on poor David was sitting quietly taking everything in his stride and even though we are the best of friends he is one of the most skeptical people I know, he doesn't believe in anything paranormal but despite this it has never affected our friendship, so I thought it only fair to him that we get ready to make our exit, just then the manager of the bar came over to see where most of his staff had disappeared to, he wasn't confrontational or hostile just kindly asked the ladies to return to work which of course they did.

As we were leaving Angie came up to me, hugged me and thanked me for all that I had told her. She said it meant so much to her in a way that I would never realize. Just to hear her words made me appreciate that I had made the right decision approaching her.

As we left the bar and were walking to get a taxi David turned to me and said I really am amazed at what I've just seen, you know how cynical I am and I can't explain it but you done a good job. Now to hear that endorsement from David was a real turn up for the books for me and even though he will always be a disbeliever it was good to know that I had given him food for thought.

Chapter 19

Jamaica

The Psychic Nerd

In the summer of 2004 the three of us went on a family holiday to Jamaica. We stayed in a fantastic hotel located right on the beach, and the hotel itself had every amenity you could imagine. In the grounds of the hotel there was a traditional Jamaican restaurant and in this location were quaint little market stands selling traditional Jamaican goods and there was also a Jamaican fortune teller who we noticed was always attracting quite a crowd every day of the week.

We would regularly walk past this gentleman on our daily walk to the beach and his appearance was very typical Jamaican with long dreadlocks, traditional robes and he wore lots of bead and other jewelry. I must admit as soon as I heard his voice I knew instantly that I would book to have a reading with him, his voice was very hypnotic. Another reason I was so keen to have a reading was due to the fact that voodoo is commonplace in Jamaica and many of the other Caribbean Islands so with this in mind I was keen to learn about this practice and was prepared for anything during my reading.

I left Helen and Lucas playing in the pool whilst I went to meet the fortune teller at a pre-booked appointment, like I said he always appeared very busy and readings were by appointment only. As I entered the "tent" for my reading I must admit he was very intimidating, even sitting down he seemed huge; I'm tall and not easily intimidated but there was just something daunting about him.

He remained seated as I walked in and he just sat staring at me, as if he was staring right through my eyes to the back of my skull. After a few seconds he gestured for me to sit down and he finally broke his stare but not his silence.

After what seemed like an eternity but was probably only a couple of minutes he finally started nodding his head at me and when he spoke he told me I had special skills which I would learn to use more and more as I grew older, he also explained to me that what I had encountered during my childhood was my introduction to my psychic abilities and should look back at it as a positive experience. I was blown away that he knew all this before I had even uttered a word!

He then went on to give me very accurate information about my family, my career and also predictions about my future many of which have come to fruition over the years since then, one of which included a move overseas which at that time was never on my radar.

The Psychic Nerd

He then asked me if I wanted to carry out a simple psychic test with him which of course I agreed to more out of curiosity than anything else. He immediately produced a notepad and a psychic text book of some description which were located on the floor behind him. He wrote something on the notepad which I could not see, then asked me to choose 2 numbers ranging from 1-15. I selected the numbers, the first two that at that popped into my head, he then asked me to tell him the numbers I had chosen. As I told him the numbers he lifted his notepad and written clearly were the 2 numbers that I had selected. He then started to laugh as though he knew he was correct before I even confirmed it. His laugh was loud, deep and booming that seemed to emanate from his very inner core and his whole body shook.

He then opened the book at a chapter about different types of psychic abilities. He matched the numbers that I had selected to sections in the chapter and then began to read aloud what I quickly realized was a description of different types of psychic abilities. He explained to me that the numbers I had randomly selected were related to the abilities that I was capable of, he added that I was more than capable of all these skills I just needed to develop my sensitivity and sharpen my tools in order to progress but I was more than capable of doing so.

He then passed me his business card and asked me to keep in touch with him on this journey as he thought it would be useful to have someone to offer advice along the way. I was a little overwhelmed by his generous offer and indeed everything he had just revealed to me, however I took his card, shook his hand and thanked him for everything. As I was leaving he said to me Robert each one of us is an individual consciousness and sometimes it can take a lifetime to develop, trust me when I tell you that you do not need to take that long.

Walking back to my hotel room, going over our meeting together it sudden occurred to me that once again I had been given a validation of my capabilities; just how many times did I need to receive these affirmations before I would truly accept what I was capable of? It was definitely a time to take a step into the unknown.

Chapter 20

Street Psychic

The Psychic Nerd

One Saturday evening several months later I was out with some male friends having a catch up in the bars in the famous Matthew Street in Liverpool. Now for those of you not familiar with Matthew Street, it's the home of the Cavern Club where The Beatles were discovered and it also home to many other bars, pubs and clubs. One such pub, and one of our regular haunts, (perhaps not the best phrase for this book) was The Grapes. The Grapes was often frequented by The Beatles as back in the 1960's it was the only traditional pub on Matthew Street that served alcohol as the Cavern Club at that time was alcohol free and The Beatles used to have a pint or two between gigs in The Grapes.

To say that this pub hasn't changed much in the past 40 years is not exaggeration and the pub has become somewhat of a shrine to The Beatles but it always has a good mix of friendly locals and fans from all over the world and is a great destination to enjoy a few beers with friends.

Anyway back to the night in question. I had only had a couple of drinks, it was still pretty early in the evening and the pub was exceptionally busy so I decided to go outside and get some fresh air telling my friends I would be back in a couple of minutes. As soon as I stepped outside almost instantly I was drawn to a man and woman, but more so the woman, who were standing about 5 feet away from me.

They were just standing together talking and after a couple of minutes the man walked away.

Just to explain, when I have this feeling of being drawn to someone it's like a magnet, the pull is instant and it is as though I am being physically pulled over to the person in question. Usually when this does happen I know that someone is trying to push through usually with a message for this person. Despite this happening to me on numerous occasions, it is never easy approaching a complete strangely as they either think you are a) hitting on them, b) a complete lunatic or c) both!!

So after debating with myself whether or not to approach this woman, I decided to go over and introduce myself to her, firstly letting her know that I had seen her with her husband and I wasn't chatting her up and secondly what I was about to tell her didn't make me mad. With all bases covered I told her that I was psychic and would she mind if I spoke to her about her sister. She appeared quite accepting of my introduction but before I got any further her husband returned.

His wife explained to him who I was and I could tell he was extremely skeptical just by the look on his face. She went on to tell him that I was about to talk to her about her sister when he abruptly of this rubbish.

He then added if you are that good tell me which sister you are talking about as she has two. Now as I have mentioned previously, people are entitled to their opinion and if someone declines my approach I always thank them and walk away and sensing his hostility I was just about to do this. However at the exact moment he cynically asked this question I had an image of a little white dog walking with a woman, who I knew to be her sister, and they were walking on a beach, which I knew to be in the South of England. So I turned to her husband and said the sister I am referring to lives in the South of England, close to the sea and she has a little white dog.

The look on his face was priceless, he was totally shocked by what I had just said and I really didn't need any further validation than this but his wife confirmed that everything I had told them was

100% accurate. Quite rightly she was a little puzzled as to why I had received this image/message for her as her sister was still alive. My best way of explaining this to her was that even though I did not have a definitive message someone wanted me to connect her with her sister for reasons unbeknown to me. I suggested that she should give her a call as she may require some help or assistance or quite simply she may just need to hear a friendly voice. She assured me that she would do just that.

At this point my friends came to see where I had disappeared to and we were moving on to a new venue. As I was leaving her husband approached me and said I've always been skeptical about such things but after tonight I will most definitely be more open-minded and trust me when I tell you that we will most definitely make that phone call. It was quite a turnaround from one so disbelieving and it was uplifting to hear it.

I too often wondered if there was a reason for my connection with this couple on that night however I am certain that just by speaking with them did indeed serve the purpose for which it was intended.

Chapter 21

Man's Best Friend

The Psychic Nerd

Man's Best Friend and our beautiful boxer dog Tasha certainly was that. She was a much loved member of our family for 12 years. She was loyal, faithful and protective of us all. From the very first day Helen and I brought her home as a tiny puppy she was a mischievous, spirited bundle of energy who loved long daily walks regardless of the weather.

She was fit and healthy for 12 years, and then almost overnight her health failed rapidly. We took her to the vet and she was diagnosed with heart failure, the vet prescribed her with medication which she hoped would prolong her life expectancy but there was no guarantee. We agreed to monitor her and should there be any deterioration in her condition we would indeed bring her back to see the vet.

From that first consultation Tasha never truly recovered and within the space of 3 days Helen and I knew that sooner rather than later we had an agonizing decision to make. That same evening, Helen rang the vet and she told us to bring Tasha over as soon as possible warning her that the prognosis wasn't good. It was never our intention that she would suffer but having to make the decision to have her euthanized was one of the hardest choices we have ever made.

Thankfully Lucas aged 8 at this time, was fast asleep in bed, blissfully unaware of what was happening. Helen and I agreed that I would take Tasha to the vets and as I carried her to the car it broke my heart as I watched Helen saying her final farewell to our beloved Tasha. It obviously didn't get any better and when I arrived at the surgery the vet was waiting for us and we were led directly into a consulting room. Straight away I knew it wasn't good news but the vet was so caring and compassionate and she guided me through what to expect.

I sat on the floor in the consulting room and held Tasha tightly in my arms, doing my best to comfort her and watching her as she took her last breath following the injection until she became heavy in my arms and I knew she had gone. It was one of the most difficult things I have had to do in my life. For months afterwards we often commented on how empty the house was without Tasha in it.

Now you may be wondering why I am telling you all this but several months after Tasha passed away she returned for the first of many visits.

The first time it happened I was lying on the floor in front of the fire watching TV and Helen was sitting close by on the couch. I was immediately aware of her presence next to me but I could also smell her.

I always used to say she smelled like digestive biscuits and I could absolutely smell her scent as though she was sitting right next to me, which was in fact one of her favorite spots.

I sat up and said to Helen I've just had a visit from Tasha, it was as though she was back here with me. I explained to her what had happened and that I hoped it was her way of coming back to show us she was ok. After this visit it happened to me on numerous other occasions, at different times, in different rooms of the house but always at home. Strangely enough Helen has also been visited by Tasha too on several occasions and she too picked up on her scent. She took great comfort when this happened and was always happy to think her beloved Tasha was close by.

One of the most recent visits I had from her was in March 2012 when she appeared before me with my Father and my Nan. I will elaborate in greater details later in this book.

People often wonder about pets and whether they join us in the afterlife and from my own experience I can positively say that yes they do; they are as much a part of your family here as they are in the afterlife. I hope people can take comfort from this as I know from personal experience how difficult losing a much loved pet can be.

Chapter 22

The Fridge

The Psychic Nerd

I had been to a business meeting one day which had finished earlier than scheduled so there was no-one at home when I arrived back. As soon as I opened the front door I immediately started to feel an extremely cold feeling at the bottom of my feet. The best way I can describe it was as though I had been locked inside a fridge.

Now I have to explain something about what I call my psychic radar. When my psychic radar picks something up all of my senses are instantly heightened and my abilities are ultra-sensitive and I am able to pick up on the minutest detail but on this occasion it was very different.

So as I entered the hallway, the ice cold sensation that I was feeling gradually started to creep up the whole of my body. I stood still for a couple of minutes taking stock of my surroundings with my psychic radar on full alert and I started to walk upstairs and as I walked up the stairs I was becoming colder with every step I took.

I am not exaggerating when I say by the time I was at the top of the stairs I was shivering and I could actually see my breath when I reached the landing it was as though I was standing outside in midwinter I felt so cold and I had a strange feeling in the pit of my stomach.

I knew something wasn't right but for reasons unknown to me, my psychic radar wasn't assisting me greatly at this point.

As I walked across the landed and stepped into my bedroom I was instantly embraced with the usual warmth of home however I still had that feeling of uneasiness, it wasn't a sinister feeling I just felt rather unsettled probably due to my own frustration at my inability to understand what was happening.

I walked around the rest of the house and was unaware of any other cold spots but despite this I still didn't feel especially reassured. The events that I had just experienced had left me feeling bewildered, confused and most of all somewhat perturbed as I had no idea what had happened.

After sleeping on the events of the previous day I awoke still feeling unsettled and decided that if I had the opportunity that day in work I would try and speak to Karen to ask her for some direction.

Before I had the chance to approach Karen she tracked me down and told me she had been constantly been receiving messages for me from someone who she described as being quite demanding but polite but rather obstinate and wouldn't take no for an answer.

She had repeatedly tried to switch off from these messages but hadn't been able to despite them coming through constantly. Apparently this person had been very insistent that Karen speak to me as they had tried unsuccessfully to communicate with me directly and had become somewhat irritated that I had failed to respond.

Karen then went on to give me a detailed description of an older man, which included the type of hat and the sleeve garters he wore every day both items I'm sure you'll agree are not regular everyday apparel. As soon as Karen gave me these details I instantly knew it was my maternal Granddad, Granddad Bob coming through. He told Karen that he had just wanted to say hello to me and to tell me that he was always around looking out for me and my family. She confirmed that he had tried to contact me directly and he was rather disappointed that I hadn't received his message.

I then conveyed to Karen what had happened to me the previous day and wondered if it was just a coincidence.

She assured me that it was anything but a coincidence and what had happened was a testament to the fact that my Granddad was such a strong character and despite trying everything he could in order to reach me, I hadn't been able to communicate with him. I did pick up on a powerful force at work in my home but had no idea it was him despite him doing his utmost to gain my attention which he most certainly did.

If I'm perfectly honest after this event I had mixed emotions about the whole episode.

I was elated that my Granddad had come through to Karen but by the same token I was disappointed that I hadn't connected with him; I felt as though I had failed him.

As always Karen put everything into perspective and assured me that this does happen on occasions and nevertheless I had still felt a powerful presence and somehow despite the barriers that we encountered he had still somehow managed to contact Karen, don't ask me how this happened but what I do know is that my Granddad Bob was a force to be reckoned with whilst he was alive and has certainly taken his resilient personality with him on his next journey.

Chapter 23

You Reap What You Sow

The Psychic Nerd

The anecdotes in this chapter have been related to me by Karen who conducts private readings several times per week for both groups of people and individuals and she is always highly in demand.

On one such occasion she had arranged to give a reading for a lady who lived somewhere near South Manchester. The appointment was for early evening so Karen was going immediately after she had finished work for the day. Now all psychics prepare in different ways for readings and Karen's usual preparation involved the spirits associated with her prospective client would start to make contact with Karen well before the meeting time, sometimes 24 hours or more before.

As Karen was driving to this appointment she suddenly detected the spirit of a lady in the seat next to her. The spirit told her that she was the mother of the lady she was on her way to see and she was quite insistent that she wanted to speak to Karen about her daughter. Now Karen is a very experienced psychic who is very meticulous in her practices which includes a lot or preparation prior to readings especially taking notes from spirits who visit in advance to meetings.

So bearing this in mind Karen was somewhat reluctant to start taking information from this lady from the spirit world without any method of recording it as she was driving.

Explaining this to her uninvited passenger in the car, the spirit politely requested that Karen start to take an account of what she was telling her in the notepad that she always carried with her and the spirit would ensure she arrived safely at her destination.

From that point forward Karen is adamant that she has no recollection of driving for the rest of the journey, she doesn't remember how but Karen reached her destination safely and even more bizarrely she had pages of copious notes about her imminent client she had somehow written. This is quite an incredible account which I totally believe as I know Karen to be a person of great integrity it also gives an indication of the power some spirits have is truly quite astounding.

Now this is not where this story finishes and I'm sure you are wondering what was in the notes that Karen had written, well it transpired that the spirit lady was from Jamaica and during her lifetime had practiced voodoo. The lady had on many occasions used the power of voodoo to place curses and harm people.

Apparently since she had died she had been placed in what she described as an indeterminate state, a sort of limbo which was intended to represent a form of retribution in order for her to understand the mistakes she had made using the dark skills against vulnerable people.

The spirit was very remorseful of her involvement with voodoo. She totally regretted all of her actions and involvement with occult practices and was desperate to convey this to her daughter who she had grave concerns was beginning to dabble in the occult also.

Karen was totally stunned by these revelations and a difficult meeting ensued with her client who validated almost everything Karen told her. She was also somewhat perplexed by the warning Karen passed onto her from her departed mother. Obviously I will never know the final outcome following their meeting but I would like to hope that this woman did take heed of the advice her mother was giving to her and of course the extraordinary lengths she took to ensure she got her message through to Karen.

I think what we can all learn from this tale is that we need to consider what actions we take in life as it is pretty obvious that we will be forced to revisit the results of our actions later.

Chapter 24

A Christmas Carol

The Psychic Nerd

At this point in my personal journey I was still very much an apprentice and if there was ever a time that I was looking for proof I was capable of detecting and working with spirits this one experience for me would become the foundation stone to build from for the rest of my life.

It was early December and I was away for the weekend for Christmas celebrations. I was staying in a beautiful village in Yorkshire with a group of work colleagues. We were attending a Christmas party at a nearby hotel and due to the size of our group (approximately 35-40) some were staying in the hotel and others, including myself, were staying in nearby bed and breakfast accommodation in the same village.

The village was very picturesque with a beautiful, ancient church located within it and opposite the church was the village pub. Everywhere looked so idyllic with Christmas lights twinkling almost everywhere you looked the whole scene resembled a Christmas card.

I arrived in the village mid-afternoon, parked at the Hotel and as soon as I stepped out of the car I was immediately drawn to a very old church located across from the hotel car park and in particular to the right hand side, to the rear of the church next to a graveyard, I couldn't explain why this was so but I just was strangely absorbed by it.

Before meeting my colleagues for the party I went for a walk around the village just admiring how charming the surroundings were despite the wintry conditions and I crossed an old stone bridge which had a stream with a waterfall flowing beneath it. I can remember sitting on the bridge and despite the beauty of all my surroundings I was still inexplicably drawn to the church and always the same area and every time I looked at it I had an overwhelming feeling of sadness.

I met my colleagues at the hotel and we all enjoyed the usual Christmas dinner and festivities. At about 10.30 pm I went and sat on the old bar tables outside the hotel. Again the pull to the direction of the church was very strong, I clearly remember just staring into the darkness surrounding the church as there was very little light pollution and despite the cold, it was actually a lovely evening and I enjoyed the peace and quiet after the loud party atmosphere I had just left.

After a short time had passed I rejoined the Christmas celebrations and by now the party numbers were starting to dwindle so myself and a couple of my colleagues decided to have a final couple of drinks in the Hotel bar. When we entered the bar apart from the barman and ourselves the place was pretty much deserted.

We ordered drinks and sat at the bar and I was soon chatting to the barman about the history of the village and in particular how old some of the buildings were including the pub and the church. He was very knowledgeable and it was interesting talking to him. Quite literally mid-conversation I suddenly heard a male voice telling me to ask the barman about Rick.

The barman was standing directly in front of me drying a glass and rightly or wrongly I suddenly blurted out Rick says to say hello. As soon as I said those words the color drained from his face and he just about stopped himself from dropping the glass he was holding and it was quite obvious from his reaction that I had touched a nerve to say the very least.

He looked at me and exclaimed "Rick oh my god"! Judging by his reaction it was blatantly obvious that there was a connection with him and the voice that had spoken to me. I asked him how he knew

Rick and by now the barman was visibly shaken, he struggled to get the words out but he told me that Rick was his best friend who had died six months earlier. As soon as he told me this information I asked him if Rick was buried at the right hand side of the graveyard at the back of the church. The barman confirmed he was buried at that exact location and his funeral service had taken place in the village church.

After checking with the barman to see if he was ok, he assured me he was fine and he asked if I had any further information about Rick. I told him that Rick has just pushed through to confirm his presence and that all was fine. The barman then told me that Rick's wife and young daughter lived just around the corner.

Whilst the information that was being relayed was irrelevant to me and I seemed to be throwing a long list of random names, locations, dates and even bizarre references that I had no clue as to what they were but I later found out they were specific to the Yorkshire region, these messages not only served as accurate validation but also in my opinion was Rick's way of confirming that he was still around for his loved ones even though his passing had been sudden and unexpected.

The Psychic Nerd

Gradually communication from Rick began to wane and after he left us we discussed what had just happened as it had taken us all by surprise. The barman posed the question as to whether he should speak with Rick's wife about this encounter and the best advice that I could offer him was that if she had an open mind in relation to such matters then he should most definitely tell her.

Rick had come through for a reason and in my opinion that reason was to let his loved ones know he was still there for them and always would be.

The whole episode had a rather profound effect on us all; it was sad to think of a young man in the prime of his life taken away from his family without warning and I knew that they faced a difficult Christmas, their first without him and hoped my contact with him would give them a glimmer of comfort.

When the bar closed my colleagues, myself and the barman started to walk over the old bridge back towards our bed and breakfast accommodation. As we stepped onto the bridge I immediately saw the figure of a woman dressed in a long black dress with a long white apron over it and a white bonnet mad of lace on hear head.

I stopped in my tracks at first thinking it was someone in fancy dress heading home from a Christmas celebration, she continued walking past me in a rather hurried fashion in the direction of the hotel where we had celebrated earlier making no eye contact whatsoever. I looked behind me back to the bridge and she was nowhere to be seen.

The barman who was walking next to me seen me swivel around rather abruptly and asked me what was wrong. I told him what I just seen and described every detail, he was totally shocked and then proceeded to tell me that numerous people had reported seeing the ghostly figure on the bridge for a long time. He could not believe the information he had been given by me in relation to his friend and now the lady on the bridge.

Perhaps my psychic ability was heightened that weekend hence my fleeting encounter with a ghost from Christmas past.

Chapter 25

Angels

Earlier in the book I mentioned that Karen belonged to a spiritual circle and much to my delight I was invited to attend one of their group meetings which I must admit I was both excited and somewhat apprehensive about. The meeting was scheduled for the evening and the location on this occasion was in a semirural location midway between Liverpool and Manchester.

On the day of the meeting I had scheduled a day off work and had planned to spend the morning browsing an assortment of book shops in Southport on the lookout for some I.T. related books. Upon entering the third bookshop I had a quick peruse of the I.T. section but there was nothing that took my interest and before I knew it I was looking at an area of the shop devoted to Angels. Now when I say a devoted area I would not be exaggerating if I said this display of books, posters and statues were quite shrine-like in appearance and in my opinion it seemed quite out of place in the middle of a book shop.

In the middle of the display was a very distinctive poster with an image of an angel which really caught my attention as it was so striking. I selected a book and was quickly engrossed in it and had read 2-3 chapters before I knew it. I quickly put the book back on the shelf and left the shop.

When I left the book shop angels were the only thing on my mind and I wondered if it was a signal of some sort. My curiosity was getting the better of me so I rang Karen and explained to her about the angels and since my encounter in the book shop I had been unable to clear them from my mind. Karen just started to laugh; telling me things would be clear at the meeting later.

I arrived at the circle meeting later that evening; the house was very large with what appeared to be a converted garage which had been made into an office. From what I understood the lady who owned the house conducted readings, therapies and consultations so this was where she worked from.

I knocked on the door and was invited in, Karen was already there most of the other members of the group, and as soon as I entered the meeting room I was absolutely shocked to see the whole of the room was adorned in angel memorabilia; I'm not overstating when I tell you that everywhere I looked all I could see were statues or images of angels and to top it all off the poster I had seen earlier in the book shop had been replicated onto the main wall of the room as a wall painting.

These keepsakes had not been displayed for my benefit they were part of the everyday décor of the room, it was quite a collection most of which I had been privy to earlier than expected.

It was obviously an endorsement from the spirit world and perhaps a pertinent message for me on how to hear my angels.

After the initial angelic surprise, I was introduced to all the members of the circle and I was taken aback at the energy that I could feel within the room it was almost tangible and I was eager for the meeting to commence.

The meeting was started by Julia whose home we were in and she was leading the meeting for the evening. She began by reciting the Lord's Prayer and following this she instructed us all to visualize a white light entering our bodies from the head downward and then asked us to place our hands on the table but not touching, which is something usually only depicted in the movies. The projection of white light was to protect us from any harm and it certainly worked. Julia then invited the spirits to make their presence known at which point a rumbling noise and vibration started above us and appeared to be going across the ceiling from one corner of the room to the corner of the room where we were all sitting. I nearly jumped out my chair it was so loud and I hadn't expected it.

Julia explained to me that the spirits were with us and this was the same sign they used all the time to show their presence. The best way I can describe the noise is as though someone was rolling around a heavy ball on the floor above us. As I said I was startled when I first heard the noise as it totally caught me off guard but I quickly became accustomed to it and the sound gradually diminished to more like a constant rumble in the background for the whole evening.

For me the room quickly started to fill up with many different spirits; after a few minutes the power and presence of the spirits around me seemed to increase dramatically and I began to feel an intense heat around my neck and shoulders and at the same time the spirits appeared to be spinning around in front of me. I could actually feel the gentle gusts of wind emanating from this spinning, it was very warm and felt rather soothing.

I then felt a very strong presence to my left which I knew immediately was my paternal grandmother, my Nan. At that precise moment a lady across from me told me I had a spirit standing next to me on my left side. She went on to describe my Nan so accurately right down to the support bandage she always wore on her knee. She gave me a message to say that she was always watching over me, she was proud of my success and was glad to have helped me with my early stages in I.T.

Now to most people this would be a rather insignificant message however it meant so much to me as it was from a small legacy left to my from the Nan that enabled me to buy my first ever computer at the tender age of 16 so this was quite a confirmation, not that I needed it. My Nan has many mentions in this book with more to come, which only proves in my mind how important she was to me when she was alive and still to this day is with me in spirit.

Other members of the group then came forward with various messages from different spirits with such precision of details it was mind blowing and for me it was very enlightening to just watch and learn how they communicated with the spirits. These messages sometimes came through for other circle members, family members, friends and work colleagues and they continued this for the best part of an hour. It was always the aim of the circle members to pass on these messages to the intended recipient if they were open to it, which understandably wasn't always the case.

Julia then brought out a Ouija board which they used regularly however I felt most uneasy the minute it was placed on the table; they are something I have always steered clear of as they have always had sinister connotations in my opinion. I immediately voiced my concerns and both Karen and Julia reassured me that we were all protected within the circle and there was nothing to worry about.

Rather reluctantly I agreed and the first question that was posed to the Ouija board was one about me, probably before I had an opportunity to change my mind. I cannot recall the specifics of the question all I can recollect is that it was a question about my future. Each one of us had a finger placed gently on top of the glass, and I can assure you no-one around that table was applying any pressure to the glass and it suddenly spelled out AUSTRALIA97. Not one person, including Karen, had any idea of my intention to emigrate to Australia. Indeed the whole process was in the very earliest of stages and we had only told our closest family members and friends at this time.

I obviously understood the significance of Australia but I was unsure about the 97 connection. Lucas was born in 1997 so the number had an important connection to me but I didn't really understand how it was associated to AUSTRALIA 97.

Nonetheless I have to admit I was very impressed with the result of my first Ouija board encounter. However I only agreed to use it as it was within a controlled environment and despite this I still do question the need to use them. In my experience you can communicate with spirits directly without using a Ouija board as I truly believe the misuse of these boards can open the door to sinister entities and spirits that nobody would ever want around them. I was happy when it was put away for the night and before I knew it the evening had come to an end.

I chatted with everyone before I left and thanked them all for allowing me into their circle for the evening. Interestingly each one of them told me they had noticed an increased level of spiritual activity that evening and all put it down to my attendance which was quite an endorsement.

My night with the circle was an unforgettable experience. The messages, the constant noise and the energy we all experienced as a group just goes to prove how powerful forces can be when working together.

Chapter 26

The Last Lift

The Psychic Nerd

In 2007 a good friend of mine James passed after a short illness and at the time of his passing he was only in his late 30's. James was such a kind and considerate man; the best way to describe him would be as a gentle giant. We both had a common interest in weight training, we used to meet up regularly at the gym and encourage each other during our workouts.

James and I met through my best friend David. James was the partner of David's sister and when we met we hit it off instantly. The 3 of us and our respective partners socialized together regularly and for a considerable time life was good for James, his partner Laura and their beautiful young daughter whom he absolutely adored.

Unfortunately James had a few setbacks in his life and he started to drink heavily which sadly resulted in the breakup of his relationship with Laura. Over the following years despite numerous attempts of trying to help himself and offers of help from his family and friends his health rapidly deteriorated due to a combination of a pre-existing health condition and his drinking.

I'm sorry to admit that during this time we lost contact though David and Laura regularly informed me of how he was keeping. On one such occasion David contacted me to tell me James had been admitted to hospital and his prognosis was very poor.

David and I visited him in the hospital, he was unconscious and we were both saddened and shocked to see him so fragile and helpless a shadow of his former self; it was very hard to think of how he had been just a couple of years earlier. We visited him on a couple more occasions but sadly he never regained consciousness and he passed away a few days later.

Despite their separation Laura offered her love and support to James every step of the way right to the very end which included organizing his final farewell. The funeral service was held at his local church and following this we proceeded to a nearby cemetery for his burial. As I was parking my car at the cemetery I said to Helen I have a feeling Laura is going to need me to help carry the coffin. Helen was somewhat surprised at my statement especially as at the church there had been 6 pallbearers but before she even had a chance to respond Laura approached me and I knew what the question was going to be before she even asked but when she did I accepted without hesitation.

As I lifted the coffin onto my shoulders with the other pallbearers I can remember thinking to myself about the weight training we used to do and that this would be the last lift we would ever do together and as we carried him to his final resting place I reflected on how I should have done more for James during his troubled times; a decision which I totally regret to this day.

Helen and I regularly keep in contact with Laura and her daughter who has grown into a wonderful young lady and I know James would be extremely proud of her.

James had always been aware of my spiritual ability and he too had an interest in the subject. I have often wondered why James has never made contact with me even just to say hello or somehow make his presence known. I have asked myself this question on numerous occasions whenever of a family member or friend unfortunately passes away and I am afraid that is a question I do not have the answer to. All I can wish for is that James is at peace now and one thing I am certain of is that he will be watching over his beautiful daughter.

Chapter 27

The Peaceful Hour

The Psychic Nerd

Working in the I.T. industry I would often be working late on projects burning the midnight oil and I would listen to the local radio station in Liverpool, my favorite show was a late night talk show hosted by a DJ called Pete Price. The final hour of the show was called The Peaceful Hour and it had quite a following in Liverpool.

(Incidentally I am going to send a copy of this book to Pete Price as I know he has a very keen interest in this subject and it will be interesting to see what he thinks of it all).

A regular visitor on this show was a psychic medium called Phoebe who is very gifted in her spiritual abilities and skills. I would regularly listen to her giving readings live on-air for callers to the show.

One night I decided to call in myself for a reading, and after numerous attempts I managed to get on the show. Now at that time I was personally experiencing some confidence problems which I know everybody can encounter from time to time.

Phoebe began my reading and immediately told me I was a very spiritual person and I had psychic skills which I would fully embrace in the future.

She spoke about some of my childhood experiences and also told me that she saw a move for myself and my family to Australia all of which was accurate.

After receiving such a precise reading I was ready for Phoebe to bring the call to an end when she suddenly hesitated before asking me why I was having a confidence crisis. I was quite taken aback when she asked me this and before I could reply she reassured me that I had absolutely no foundation for my concerns and I should immediately dispel any self-doubt I was experiencing, she went on to explain my career would flourish considerably.

I can emphatically confirm that the reading Phoebe gave me was very accurate and indeed gave me the shot in the arm I was looking for. Later that year after a lengthy application we did in fact finally emigrate to Australia. This was one of the most nerve racking and stressful processes I have ever experienced. Despite the promise of exciting new beginnings it's very daunting to sell your home, pack up all your possessions, quit perfectly good jobs and then take your wife and child away from wonderful family and much loved friends to move to another country half way across the world.

Both Helen and I had our fair share of uncertainty about our move and even 7 years on we still are unsure if this will be the last country we will chose to live in. However for the most part we have had very positive experiences and as Phoebe predicted since arriving in Australia my career in the I.T. industry has indeed flourished and I have worked in some very high level positions across varied large players in the industry. I do not think I would have had such opportunities if I had stayed in the United Kingdom at this point in time.

Chapter 28

New Beginnings

The Psychic Nerd

After all the trials and tribulations we encountered prior to our emigration, we finally bid a tearful farewell to our loved ones in the UK and all 3 of us arrived in Perth, Western Australia positive for our future life together on the other side of the world. In the first instance my priority was to make sure we all settled well into our new country and I decided to hold back on continuing with my spiritual journey.

Less than 6 months after our arrival I'd successfully gained employment, we'd bought a new home in a beautiful coastal suburb, Lucas was extremely happy in his new primary school and Helen was enjoying taking being a full time stay at home Mum since Lucas was a baby.

One Saturday afternoon I was driving home from the local shops when I noticed a banner at the side of the road advertising a psychic fair literally a five minute drive from our home. As soon as a I read the sign and realized it was being held that day I decided to make a quick detour and go to see what was on offer.

As in all walks of life there are groups of people that exist purely to take advantage of vulnerable people. Unfortunately these people operate within the psychic medium world and dilute the good work legitimate psychics and mediums are involved in. One such example of this type of bad practice is when these so called psychics constantly ask leading questions which they are well practiced in, which then enable them to extract information unwittingly from the person having the reading. To me this information should be forthcoming from the spiritual side and not be obtained under false pretenses. In my opinion a large majority of the people attending these events are usually rather vulnerable and seeking solace and unfortunately due to this they are often preyed upon by unscrupulous charlatans who often given the genuine psychic mediums a bad reputation.

So getting back to the psychic fair, as soon as I entered the venue I could immediately feel the energy radiating around me. The venue was a large hall with a smaller annex leading off it and rather than just approaching the first psychic I stumbled upon for a reading, I made the conscious decision to take a more measured approach and wait to see if I was guided to a certain psychic. If no-one stood out to me I would leave without having a reading.

The Psychic Nerd

In both rooms there were approximately 25-30 people offering psychic readings, mediumship, Reiki healing and tarot card readings to name but a few! I glanced around the venue ignoring the hum of energy I was instantly picking up on and walked slowly around pondering what each person had to offer. I left the main hall, entered the annex and I found myself at a stand that contained various items including some very distinctive patterned cloth which attracted my attention immediately. A lady was standing next to me who picked up the fabric and I remarked to her how appealing the pattern was. She turned to me smiled and nodded her agreement then placed the fabric back on the table and walked away. I continued to look around the remaining stands and returned into the main hall at which point I immediately noticed the lady who had been holding the fabric and she was now sitting at a table offering psychic readings and she was staring across at me; the deal was done and I instinctively knew she was the one. I was aware that this was just another little nudge in the right direction from the spirit world.

I approached her and she invited me to sit down and we agreed on a thirty minute reading. Her name was Susie and at this point my spiritual radar was sitting very comfortably and I felt totally relaxed.

Initially the only question Susie asked was my name and she then stared intently into my eyes for what felt like an eternity without uttering a word. Ordinarily this would have made me feel a little disconcerted however I was totally at ease, which is always a good indicator for me.

Susie explained to me that since I had approached her she could feel an immense heat emanating from my body, I didn't feel any different so it was quite surprising to hear.

Almost immediately she confirmed that I was very psychic and once again she confirmed that I had immense skills which I was barely tapping into, and obviously she wasn't the first person to tell me this. I listened attentively to what she was telling me occasionally nodding, not wanting to give anything away.

Bearing this in mind, Susie then brought up the topic of past lives; a subject I must admit I know very little about however Susie assured me that I had lived a number of past lives and she took me right back to Egyptian times and could clearly see me performing some type of magic or sorcery whilst dressed in a rather dramatic ensemble which included distinctive headgear which she explained in great detail. She mentioned various other past lives I had lived through the ages including a warrior, and several lives as military men. It was fascinating to hear her describe all this to me and it was quite an eye opener to say the least.

Throughout my reading Susie was constantly fanning herself and exclaiming how hot she felt just from the heat I was generating and how she had never before experienced anything like this. This brought Susie back to the subject of my psychic ability and she enquired what, if anything, had I done to enhance or develop my skills. As briefly as possible I gave Susie an overview of some of my experiences to date, including how Karen had mentored and advised me from the very start of my psychic development and indeed Susie concurred with everything that Karen had previously told me and she urged me to develop the gifts that I had at my disposal. We discussed various methods I could use in order to enhance my abilities and Susie also suggested I practice meditation as she thought it would be benefit me greatly. She also suggested looking around locally for a spiritual group or church that I could attend.

When Susie concluded the reading it had lasted for over an hour and 20 minutes, I offered to cover the cost of the extra time I had taken up but she refused telling me to forget about it as she had really enjoyed the reading. I too had thoroughly enjoyed the reading and for the first time I actually felt excited for the future development and enhancement of my psychic abilities. I had yet again received further endorsement of my skills from a very experienced psychic medium; how many more validations would I need before I began to have the confidence in my talent?

Chapter 29

A Friend Comes Calling

The Psychic Nerd

This chapter is rather short but very interesting nonetheless. It shows that spirits can come calling anytime and quite unexpectedly.

At home one evening both Helen and Lucas were already asleep and I was working late on an important project which I was keen to deliver before the scheduled deadline. Rather than work in my study I opted to sit at the dining room table with my laptop; the house was very quiet with exception of the tapping of my keyboard and music playing quietly in the background.

After being absorbed in my work for several hours I quite suddenly sensed something or someone standing in very close proximity to me so close in fact it was making the hairs on my arms stand up. Instinctively I looked around the room but there was nothing out of the ordinary to see however I could definitely feel a presence.

Immediately my senses were heightened and I sat back in my chair, closed my eyes and waited. Strange as it may sound I suddenly I felt as though I had been placed in a wind tunnel, the force of the wind propelling around me was extremely strong and my whole body seemed to be fighting against it. Rather than try to oppose this force I tried to stay calm, I remained seated and closed my eyes, still sensing the presence nearby. As soon as I closed my eyes the name Jed came into my mind. I had known a guy back in Liverpool when I was younger called Jed, he was the older brother of one of my friends and unfortunately a couple of years earlier he had committed suicide. Upon receiving his name I opened my eyes and I could quite clearly see his spectral figure standing before me. Out loud I said hello to him, he did not respond verbally or physically but straightaway I felt such an overwhelming peacefulness and gradually the intensity of the wind began to dissipate until it completely stopped and at the same time the shadowlike figure disappeared before me. I have no idea why Jed appeared to me that night but then again there doesn't always have to be a reason sometimes they just use the psychic as a vessel to make contact for reasons not always known to the psychic. I can only hope that it helped Jed in some way at least.

Strangely enough, despite the force of the wind I had encountered during this experience not one of the documents I had been working with had been disturbed, they had not moved an inch. A couple of weeks later I was discussing this event with a psychic friend who before I had the opportunity to tell her who had appeared to me, she suddenly blurted out the name Jed!! We were both a little taken aback at her accuracy as it's rather an unusual name which she said just sprung into her mind. Perhaps Jed was still making his presence known in a less dramatic way to both of us.

Chapter 30

Dark Forces

The Psychic Nerd

We have heard stories in this book of good and evil spirits which to me basically come down into two categories of dark and light forces. This chapter tells the story of my first introduction to dark forces since what I experienced during my childhood.

At this time the company where I was working had large open plan office space, no-one had their own office and at any time there could be about 15-20 people present in this huge space. There was one particular woman who worked for this company and whenever she was in the office I would often see dark shadows around her. For the purposes of this chapter I will refer to her as Julie.

From the start I knew these shadows had a sinister association and I would see them regularly and often before I knew Julie was even in the office. I tried to keep my distance and remain professional however following an office re-organization Julie was relocated and ended up sitting opposite me. As you can imagine every time I looked in her direction, and it was almost impossible not to, all I would see would be these dark, depressing shadows looming around her. After several months of working in this environment I must admit the feeling of having these ominous, shadowy figures constantly present was making me feel rather wretched and despondent so I felt when I had an appropriate opportunity I would speak to Julie, tactfully of course. The opening came late one afternoon when most of our colleagues had left for the day, I was making a coffee when Julie walked into the staff room too. Turning to speak to her I said Julie do you mind if I ask you a question, she said she didn't object so I just fired the question to her asking why she had all these dark shadows around her. She didn't appear shocked at all at my question; indeed she looked right back at me and laughed before replying the same reason you have all the white light around you, at which point we both started laughing.

Now despite seeing these dark shadows constantly around Julie I did not think she was dark herself, these shadows were around her but I did not really mean she was cut from the same cloth. My initial question opened a dialogue between us, we grabbed a coffee and we chatted at length about spirituality, dark practices and magical arts. It transpired that when she was younger Julie had foolishly (her words not mine) experimented in what is commonly referred to as black magic and she had practiced black magic against people in her life at that time and was very regretful of these acts now.

I really did believe Julie was truly remorseful of her past actions; regardless of her previous deeds she too was a very spiritual person and when we initially chatted despite our initial differences we surprisingly had a lot in common. Julie stated that she regularly seen spirits walking alongside me though I am happy to report they were not dark shadows/spirits.

Thereafter Julie and I would often get together and discuss a variety of topics including spirituality, black and white magic, psychic mediums to name but a few. In fact it was Julie who introduced me to the term psychic drain and what it meant.

In the most simplistic of terms people with psychic ability can if they are not careful take onboard the feelings of people around them in a negative way, in other words if you have someone next to you who is feeling really low this can manifest itself onto you as a psychic which is not good. This can actually result in the person who generated the feelings actually feeling better because the negativity is passed onto the psychic. Julie taught me how to put up barriers to block the drain from happening whenever necessary and how on occasions when required how to use my psychic ability to avoid situations that could result in me becoming low or depressed, it was a valuable skill to acquire and one which I have used on many occasions.

Whenever Julie and I met for a discussion we had to limit the amount of time we could spend together on a one to one basis. This was due to the fact that we would be inundated by spirits just dropping in and letting their presence be known to us both. The energy generated during these occasions was pretty mind blowing and I could best describe it as though Julie and I were spirit magnets; it was a bit like Piccadilly Circus for spirits. During such meetings an intense pressure would build in my head which would become almost unbearable and I would usually only be able to last for about twenty to thirty minutes. There was definitely something about the dynamics between us that ignited such a reaction. I have often asked Julie if she has tampered with the dark arts since her earlier years and she assured me she hadn't, however she definitely has a mischievous streak within her and I wonder if there will ever be an occasion when her curiosity will lead her back to her former practices.

Chapter 31

They Just Push Through

The Psychic Nerd

I mentioned earlier about detecting when someone has a low mood, regardless of whether they are trying to conceal their feelings, I am able to pick it up instantly. One such instance I was finishing lunch at a local café and was preparing to leave when a colleague called Collette came in. She spotted me and asked if I wanted a coffee with her; despite my planned departure I instantly detected her despondency, even though she appeared to be happy enough I could tell it was a façade. She brought the coffees over and we chatted about the weather and other such mundane topics for several minutes when I asked her what was bothering her as she appeared to be extremely unhappy.

Initially she denied that her mood was low however the feeling of sadness she was emanating was so strong that it was almost tangible. At the same time I was aware of a spirit attempting to push through. Now Collette had no idea about my psychic ability, as it really isn't something I have ever made public but I was almost 100% certain that whoever was attempting to push through was somehow connected to Collette. Therefore as briefly as I could I told Collette a little about my skills and how I was sure that someone in the spirit world was coming through for her and despite being rather shocked at my revelation she was enthusiastic to learn what I had to say.

Opening my thoughts to whoever was pushing through straightaway my mind was filled with the picture of a young man with dark hair, a perfect beaming smile and to be truthful he was so handsome he could have been a male model. As I described him to Collette I could see him quite clearly standing in bright sunshine.

Collette was quite upset as soon as she heard my description of this young man and she asked me if I knew his name; I asked him for his name and instantly he said Simon. I repeated this to Collette and she burst into tears, she was inconsolable for several minutes and when she did compose herself Colette explained to me Simon was her best friend who had died just a couple of years earlier in tragic circumstances when he was just 27. She then took out her purse and inside was a photograph which to my utter amazement was the exact image I had seen of Simon – a very handsome young man, dark hair, perfect smile and he was standing alone with the sun shining in the background.

Collette too was stunned by both the accuracy of my description of Simon and also the confirmation of his name. She explained to me how just receiving this message from him had put her problems into perspective and had given her a much needed boost just to hear from him.

This account shows how loved ones who have passed away still watch over us and love us just as they did when they were alive. Of course it is not always possible for them to push through as Simon did but they do it in ways that we often dismiss as coincidence or peculiarity but that's not always the case don't dismiss your instincts as more often than not they are correct. Loved ones can send us a message of love and support when we least expect it and in the most unusual ways. Everything comes to you at the right moment. Be patient.

Chapter 32

The Young Girl

The Psychic Nerd

If I was ever looking for some proof of what can be achieved on a psychic level I would say what I am about to tell you is that proof. Following on from the advice I received from Susie at the psychic fair to develop my skills I found a group at a local spiritualist church and I attended my first meeting one Sunday evening

As I walked into the church there were already quite a few people present, all the chairs were arranged in a circular formation and before I was even seated my attention was immediately drawn to a lady sitting at the front of the church, I picked up a welcoming vibration from her instantly – I later found out her name was Nicky.

The formation of the chairs was not how I had imagined them to be, I was expecting them to be similar to pews as per a conventional church and I was hoping to discretely slide into a pew, watch and learn and hopefully remain under the radar, at least for my first meeting. Believe it or not I am a rather shy person so for me seeing this large circle of chairs with everyone facing each other was a rather daunting prospect for me. Self-consciously I took a seat and waited for the proceedings to commence.

Nicky introduced herself and welcomed everyone into the light of the church, she also introduced a male psychic medium who was the guest for the evening and was apparently well known within the local spiritual community in Western Australia. Nicky explained that this particular evening was a circle night which occurred approximately every 4 weeks during which involved meditation and a lot more readings than a regular service.

Upon hearing how the evening would evolve I must admit my initial self-consciousness evaporated and I eagerly waited for events to commence.

There were about 20 of us present and the service started with a blessing. The guest medium then began by talking to the audience which included several personal readings. This lasted for about 30 minutes and we then took a slightly different direction whereby all the lights were dimmed, candles lit and relaxing music playing in the background. Nicky spoke gently to the audience guiding us into a relaxed state of mind, for me this was my first introduction into meditation and I must admit I was overcome with a feeling of tranquility that I had never before experienced.

Before the meditation drew to a close Nicky requested we keep our eyes closed for a couple of minutes afterwards, she went on to explain that when we opened our eyes we may see some things that may not really make sense and regardless of this we should try to remember what we had seen in order to relate to the group following the meditation.

Nicky gradually brought us all out of our meditated state and once again she re-iterated the importance of waking up slowly and to remember any images or visions we may see.

Gradually I opened my eyes and after blinking several times I was taken aback to see standing right in front of me a young girl, aged around eleven to twelve years of age, dressed in a pretty white dress with a bright red bow tied around her waist. This little girl kept appearing in my vision coming from the right side and walking to my left side. She kept just walking in my vision right to left, right to left and always looking over her left shoulder back at me. On each occasion as she "disappeared" from my vision it was always to the left of where I was sitting towards the same group of ladies sitting in the circle.

Each time she walked in front of me I could only see the outline of her face but not her full face, the best way I can describe it was as though her face was blurred out. I tried to take in as many details as possible before she gradually vanished again to the left and this time she didn't reappear.

A few members of the group began to recount what they had seen following their meditation and I listened attentively to their interpretations some of which were very impressive. I remained silent, reluctant to share with the group what I had seen.

I suddenly felt as though I was being nudged or poked by someone or something whatever this nudge was gave me the incentive I needed and I suddenly thought you know what let's just do it and tell everyone what I had seen.

Waiting for the current speaker to finish I then raised my hand to indicate that I had something to say. Nicky nodded at me to start and I recounted to the group about the little girl and how she had stood before me always appearing from the right, walking to my left before looking over her left shoulder. I described how the little girl always walked to the direction of two older ladies sitting to my left. One of these ladies asked if I could describe the little girl to her which I did in as much detail as possible. As I was describing her the lady was nodding her head at me and when I had finished she confirmed that it sounded like the little girl was her granddaughter. I then described the dress the little girl was wearing at which point the grandmother became visibly upset which unnerved me a little and I didn't know whether to continue.

Nicky intervened and asked me to close my eyes and try to communicate with the young girl in order to obtain further information from her if possible. I did as she requested and instantly the girl appeared before me, walking slowly towards me holding a very large children's book; this book was very distinctive and was full of bright vivid colors of green, yellow and orange. The little girl held out the book to me and as she did so I could see her hands holding the book and she was pushing the book towards me as if she wanted me to take it from her.

I spoke directly to her grandmother and related to her what I had just witnessed. Again she became rather emotional upon hearing what I had to say and confirmed the book her granddaughter was showing to me was one she used to read to her at bed time. Spurred on by the accuracy of the information I was receiving, in my mind I asked the young girl for some more information. No sooner had I made this request when I felt a tremendous surge of heat overcome my body from my toes to the top of my head in seconds. The force of the heat was so strong that I was almost jolted off my seat.

As I was experiencing this, the group had witnessed me jumping from my chair and Nicky asked me what happened. I explained about the sudden intense heat that had overwhelmed me and suddenly the grandmother openly began to weep. Her friend done her best to comfort her and once she had regained her composure she revealed to us all that her 8 year old granddaughter had been burnt alive in a car crash. There was an audible intake of breath from almost everyone in the room including myself!!

Following this revelation a couple of things happened; as I said I personally was in total shock as were the rest of the group. It was apparent to us all that the intense heat I had experienced had been a validation of sorts to confirm how she had passed despite it being upsetting for us all and most distressing for her grandmother. What I had just encountered prompted a discussion between us and Nicky explained that I had been used to physically channel in part a little of what the young girl had felt when she was passing. This had never happened to me before and I must admit it was quite confronting not only to think of how horrific the death of this little girl must have been but also to realize what loved ones who have passed are capable of when trying to communicate with the family and friends they have left behind.

As our conversation continued I started to feel a penetrating heat around me, admittedly it was not as powerful as what I had initially felt and somehow it seemed like a different type of heat, however it was growing in intensity as the minutes ticked by to the point whereby the force was so strong it was as though I was being pushed forward by the heat. I was actually about to reposition myself in the room as it was quite overwhelming when a lady sitting directly opposite me unexpectedly announced that she could see a large glowing white aura around me which could account for the high temperature I once again was dealing with.

I then sensed someone standing close to me on my left hand side and instinctively I knew it was my (paternal) Nan. I then had an image of her standing at the bottom of the stairs in the house she shared with my Granddad. I took comfort from her presence, as I always do whenever she visits me and the heat slowly faded away.

The same lady opposite me then told me and the rest of the group that my grandmother was standing next to me and she commented that I had a lot of stairs to climb which to me was once again a very accurate validation as quite literally 30 seconds earlier I had just pictured my Nan standing at the foot of her stairs only now to be told this, it was anything but a coincidence. I remembered how safe I always felt as a child in the company of my Nan; being with her gave me a sense of security and well-being like no-one else and it suddenly dawned on me that perhaps that was why this little girl had come through so strongly that evening to be close once again to her grandmother.

I replayed in my mind how she had repeatedly walked in front of me, always from right to left and then looking over her shoulder at me and it was then I realized despite giving a detailed description of her I had not included her facial features as she was hiding her face from me and her face had not been clear to me when she appeared, probably due to the fact that she had been scarred by the fire when she had died.

As I began to better understand the circumstances regarding her visit I realized she too was seeking comfort from her grandmother and not so unexpectedly this time she reappeared. I told her how much she was loved and missed by her grandmother and how beautiful she was and her grandmother would never want her to hide her face away. No sooner had I given her this message when she turned to me without hiding her face and I could see her clearly before she gradually started to move away, again in the direction of her grandmother only this time she didn't look back at me and I felt she had found the peace she had come in search of.

As the evening drew to a close the grandmother came up to me to thank me for making contact with her granddaughter as just receiving a message from her had greatly reassured her that she had come through such a harrowing death. I didn't feel the need to mention about the scarring from her burns however I did assure her that in my opinion her granddaughter had also gained an inner peace which I am sure she had not had prior to contacting her grandmother that evening. Suffice to say the evening had been beneficial to both of them and I only hope it enabled them both to move on to the next stage that their path would lead them to regardless of the plane they were on.

Chapter 33

Unwanted Guests

The Psychic Nerd

Since relocating to Perth we have been very fortunate to have made some very good new friends. One such couple who we became acquainted with lived called Karen and Peter and they lived in a beautiful part of Perth very close to the beach. We had only known them for about 12 months when this episode occurred and thankfully it didn't affect our friendship in any way.

Karen and Peter had two daughters and a son who had all grown up left home but they were a very close family and they regularly came home to visit Mum and Dad. Karen works as a nurse but she is also a very accomplished practicing Reiki master.

Karen and Peter were having a get together and a barbeque at their home one Saturday evening and they were very kind enough to invite us along.

We were all having a great evening and as the night progressed discussion turned to the subject of spiritual and paranormal activities. We chatted about an assortment of topics encompassing this subject and it was refreshing to see how we all had different opinions and who believed and who was skeptical about such matters.

I noted Karen listening to what everyone had to say on this matter, she hadn't really joined in with the conversation and then quite calmly she said that she suspected there was some type of presence in her house.

She added that both she and members of her family had all caught a glimpse of shadows in the house or sensed a presence of some description within her home. As soon as Karen spoke about this it immediately took me right back to my childhood and all the untoward happenings myself and my family had encountered.

Her husband Peter, who openly admits is rather skeptical on such matters, also confirmed that he too had both sensed a presence and seen shadows throughout the house. Of course these revelations prompted much debate with everyone including myself, although I really didn't want to go into too much detail about my personal experiences as with the exception of Karen and Peter, I didn't really know anyone else particularly well. The evening gradually came to an end and as Helen and I were saying our goodbyes I mentioned to Karen that next time we visited I would be more than happy to have a walk around to see if I could pick up on anything. Karen readily agreed.

The Psychic Nerd

Now speaking from personal experience, when you have a presence in your home similar to the one Karen was describing, it will feed off the energy generated within the home. This energy can be both positive and negative which most families generate at times. Spirits that attach themselves and feed off negative energy are definitely not what we want in our homes.

Several months passed before we paid a return visit to Karen and Peter's home.

We arrived at Karen's house and before we entered I stood outside and surveyed the property. Despite it being dark outside the house was well lit up and from standing outside staring at the house I initially didn't pick up on anything. They had two front glass doors at the front of the house and as we walked up to the door I bathed myself with white light from my third eye chakra point which is approximately in the middle of your eyebrows and up a little. I subconsciously bathed myself from head to toe as I was walking up to the house.

Peter greeted us at the door and Helen walked in first and I followed. Trying my best to pick up on anything, again no alarm bells were going off as I walked down the hallway into the kitchen where other guests were congregated. We settled in for a few hours and enjoyed a delightful dinner together with good company.

After dinner Karen approached me and asked if I sensed anything since I had arrived, which I had not, but I explained this is not uncommon as sometimes spirits can keep themselves hidden from view or indeed from being sensed if they know someone with spiritual skills is present.

Karen asked if I wanted to have a look around the whole of the house to see if I could discover anything to which of course I agreed to.

Just to give you a brief description of the house, it is a large single story home with the main living/dining/kitchen area being a large open plan space. There was a smaller lounge room and a bedroom to the front of the house and the rest of the bedrooms and a study to the rear of the property. In the first instance I asked Karen where most of the activity was taking place and

The Psychic Nerd

she directed me to the rear of the house so that was where I ventured to.

Karen remained in the kitchen and I walked to the back of the house, as I approached the door to walk through this section of the house my attention was immediately diverted to the hallway to my left which took me to the direction of the front of the house. Not wishing to be distracted from where I was heading to I made a mental note to visit this area next.

I continued to my intended location, stood perfectly still, switched on my radar and waited. Nothing happened; not a sound, a movement or an inkling of any uninvited guest. I waited patiently for approximately 10 minutes without success so I decided to go to the front of the house to see if I had more success in this location – this was where I had felt drawn to when my pursuit had commenced. As I headed in this direction Karen seen me and followed me down the hallway.

Towards the end of the hallway the wall curved on a tight angle before it reached the front door, at the curved point there was a door and I stopped right at that spot and could sense something pretty strong in this location. I asked Karen if I could enter the room to which she agreed and I walked in. The room was a bedroom and as I stood in the area I was again drawn to the curved wall on the bedroom side and I knew there was considerable activity in this part of the house. I stood in the doorway of the room and began to visualize a tall male figure who was dressed in old period-style clothing and he was wearing a tall, black hat. The hat was similar to the style worn by Abraham Lincoln style and he was also wearing a cape over his shoulders, not dissimilar to what Sherlock Holmes wears. Straightaway I did get the impression that whoever this gentleman was he certainly was not overly impressed with me being there.

Apart from sensing the presence of this male, I believed there to be a huge presence of energy similar to that of a portal. Without wanting to distress her I explained to Karen what I was thinking and I indicated to her where this energy source was coming from – just above our heads.

I went on to explain to her that I would be entering this portal, it was nothing for her to fear though the light situated directly above us may flicker but that often happened in such scenarios.

The Psychic Nerd

Slowly I raised my right arm into the energy field, the power I felt surging through my body was immense then almost simultaneously as expected the light bulb started to flicker, we both looked up at the light and it was flickering on and off so rapidly I thought it may shatter. Gradually I lowered my hand and the light flickering stopped. Karen and I looked at each other rather taken aback by what had just happened. To be perfectly honest I hadn't expected such a powerful response and it confirmed our suspicions that a spirit of some description was present within Karen's home and we agreed to try and find out a little more about what we were dealing with.

We left the hallway and walked back into the bedroom at which point Karen's two grown up daughters joined us, out of curiosity more than anything else, or so I initially thought.

All four of us chatted for a few minutes about the Abraham Lincoln type character I had seen a few minutes earlier and as I was describing him in detail it was evident to me that Karen's youngest daughter had experienced numerous happenings in her home, many of which she had eluded to share with her family and understandably I could relate to her on this matter.

Not wishing to put her under any undue pressure, I tentatively broached the subject with her. She admitted to us that since moving to this house when she was in her early teens she had always uneasy feeling, particularly within this bedroom which had been her bedroom for a short period of time, until she switched bedrooms at her request. This room was now only used for guests. She went on to add that despite the Australian climate this room always felt inexplicably cold, she always sensed a presence whenever she was in the room and would often see dark shadows passing by. She admitted that she felt foolish at the time and didn't raise her fears to anyone else and it was only during the past few months that it was all coming to light and she was only now revealing all her experiences.

I explained to them it was my opinion this area was the central focus in the house and the spirit was using this area like a gateway. Karen and her daughters all confirmed that this area was where most encounters had happened so it definitely was a hot spot. Although I was picking up all these details it was clear to me that this male presence, who had been similarly described by numerous people, was not coming forward to me.

I had seen an image of him but I was unable to communicate with him. I had the distinct impression that he did not want to associate with me, although he did not in any way appear to be sinister; I genuinely felt he did not want to harm anyone. Quite truthfully if that had ever been his intention he had had plenty of opportunity to do so in the past.

When people see a ghost or spirit although they are obviously alarmed by what they have seen the ghost can also be startled too. If you think in the realm of parallel universes if somehow one can inadvertently step between them then strange inexplicable happenings may occur which is equally unfathomable to the spirit as it is for the living person.

With this in mind, and being respectful of the presence in Karen's home, I did politely ask the spirit to leave, very simply explaining that this was not his home and he should seek comfort elsewhere. This may sound rather preposterous to some non-believers however such requests in many similar cases have proven to be very successful and it was never my intention to create havoc and make the situation difficult for Karen, Peter and their family with an angry ghost and quite frankly we had nothing to lose by kindly asking him to leave and apart from an odd fright the family were living happily in their home.

Since that evening Karen has reported very few encounters from their ghostly presence. A couple of weeks later Karen's daughters invited the Western Australian Paranormal society into their home who again validated a lot of what I had detected around a male spirit wearing a large hat etc. but they also detected a second spirit too which I did not. Nonetheless the descriptions from us both were very similar despite our separate visits.

My path would cross again with Karen's younger daughter Hannah which I will illustrate in the next chapter.

Chapter 34

Spooks on the Barbie

The Psychic Nerd

Approximately a year or so had passed since our last visit to Karen and Peter's home and whilst we had met at other social gatherings over the course of this year I had not yet returned to their house.

Karen and Peter were hosting a get together with our usual group of friends and also Karen and Peter's children and their partners so all in all there was quite a houseful. This was the first time I had met with Hannah and her sister Christine and they were both keen to learn a little bit more about my past, how had I known I was psychic and in what ways I practiced my skills.

I gave them a concise overview of my childhood experiences and how this had led me to where I am today. I explained that on occasions spirits just appeared to me without warning to give a message to a loved one and at other times when people ask me for a reading I have found that holding jewelry belonging to the person asking for a reading often assists me greatly. The best way I can describe it is as soon as the jewelry touches my hand and I close my fingers over it I being to see pictures and words just start appearing in my mind.

As I was talking about this I looked to Hannah and as I did I was taken back to the 17th century and I could clearly see her dressed in full costume from that era. When I told her this she did not appear too surprised and confirmed that she had been told this before by a psychic medium.

As we were discussing this her face kept pushing out towards me, it was rather disconcerting as I had never experienced anything quite like this before. However the next image I visualized depicted Hannah being executed after being found guilty of being a witch and I was unsure whether I should tell her what I had seen so erring on the side of caution I initially explained that in this past live it would appear that she had a psychic ability and had been declared a witch. Hannah was fascinated by everything I told her and seemed to take it all in her stride. Before I had the opportunity to elaborate further she asked me if she had been executed and I confirmed that this appeared to be the case. Her partner made a lighthearted comment about this which thankfully lifted the mood and I reassured Hannah that during this period of time hundreds of women were murdered purely due to the fact that people were afraid and ignorant of the abilities that psychics possessed and unfortunately due to this lack of understanding these "witches" were executed in the most barbaric, inhumane ways.

After receiving such compelling details regarding Hannah's past life I was interested to see how tuned in she was to her psychic abilities, bearing in mind she had been very perceptive to the activities in her home. I wear 2 rings on my wedding finger which I took off and before handing them to her I explained that she should take them from me, place them in the palm of her hand and then close her fingers around the rings and concentrate on what came into her mind.

I passed her the rings off, she placed them in her palm and as soon as she closed her fingers around them she freaked out and immediately asked me to take them back; as soon as she had taken hold of the rings she had a sensation of tingling all over her upper body which had really unnerved her. I persuaded here to keep hold of the rings, close her fingers and once again try to tell me the first things that came into her head.

To be truthful she was very apprehensive so I portrayed an image in my mind and asked Hannah to try and detect exactly what I was thinking of. The image I had selected was the bridge in the village in Yorkshire that I had spoken about in an earlier chapter in this book

You have to bear in mind that we were probably not in the most conducive environment for this experiment to take place however despite getting off to a shaky start Hannah was not deterred and with a little encouragement from myself and our small audience in the kitchen she began to focus on the image I was projecting to her.

After a couple of minutes she blurted out the word bridge. I was impressed. I then asked her to describe the bridge in greater detail and without a seconds hesitation she described the bridge with great accuracy. I was very impressed.

I congratulated her on how accurate she had been and I decided to take the test a step further as I was very confident she was more than capable. I explained to her about the significance of the bridge and what had transpired at that location. I asked her to clear her mind in order to try and tell me the name of the spirit who had connected with me that evening.

Without anyone else being able to read it, I wrote the name on a piece of paper, folded it up and handed it to Karen for safekeeping and asking her not to look at it or anyone else for that matter.

I turned back to Hannah who was deep in thought concentrating intently on generating the name, after a little encouragement she said the name Warren. Not giving anything away, I asked her where she got that name from and she explained that she just kept seeing the letters RR together and she picked a name from that.

Now this is where it gets really interesting, I told her she had the wrong name but she should not be discouraged by this; I then reminded people of what she had said about seeing the letters RR together. I asked Karen to unfold the paper on which I had written two names which were Richard and Rick and I had circled both R's at the start of each name.

Hannah, Karen and our small audience were astonished when they realized how close Hannah had been in her prediction and even though she did not get the name correct the association with RR could not be denied. I was extremely impressed.

Chapter 35

The Gypsy & Reiki Healer

The Psychic Nerd

This part of my life in connection with my psychic ability and development was very interesting for me; the activities of spirits around me had been gradually increasing in activity for a while and I was doing my utmost to cultivate my gift. At around the same time I had joined a new company in Perth and my office was located just south of the city. The company had consultants from overseas flying into Perth for short to mid-term contracts. One such person was a lady named Paula who was very affable and we soon became good friends. We often had very interesting conversations covering a wide spectrum of topics.

One day we began to discuss spirituality and it transpired that Paula was a Reiki healer. We discussed at length spirituality and what she had accomplished in relation to her Reiki healing. As I was fairly new to this company I was rather reluctant to speak about my psychic skills, as unfortunately some people can be quite judgmental about such matters, so other than telling Paula I was spiritual I didn't really reveal much else.

However after a couple of months had passed I eventually told her and when I did she told me she wasn't very surprised as she had an inkling there was a little more to me than I had let on. I then gave her a brief overview of my skills, how it had started when I was a child and how I was trying to develop my abilities now.

After answering many of her questions we then started talking about a friend of hers who lived in the United Kingdom and had been having some issues with some teenage children. Now this wasn't the normal anti-social behavior type of problems, on the contrary these children were calling at her house and when she answered she would be met by 3 or 4 children all of whom had jet black eyes and on each occasion they asked if they could come into her home.

Paula confirmed that her friend always declined their request and admitted that she had a feeling of uneasiness whenever they called and without wanting to appear rude she just declined their request and closed the door on them. She had told Paula how disconcerting their eyes were and each time they had called it had really unsettled her.

As Paula was relating this account to me I remembered previously reading about gypsies who were known for having very dark black eyes and I wondered if perhaps if it was gypsy children who were worrying her friend. I tried to visualize her friend's house in my mind and I gave her an accurate description of the front door and inside the hall way and stairs. I could also see an image of the children at her door and I genuinely did not feel that they had any sinister intentions their actions were more mischievous than anything else in my opinion and Paula agreed to let her friend know she shouldn't be afraid.

Coincidentally another lady who Paula and I worked with who was named Natasha had some kind of gypsy connection though what it was exactly I could not pinpoint. Natasha too was from the UK and one day she received the news her Aunt had passed away. Apparently Natasha had been extremely close to her Aunt who had in fact raised her and she was much more like a mother figure to her than an Aunt.

Natasha flew back to the UK for the funeral and after several weeks upon her return it was obvious she had been deeply affected by her loss. I felt as though I should reach out to her as her grief was almost tangible so one afternoon I passed her a note with a very brief description of what I could do and not wanting to intrude I just told her to message me if she wanted to chat.

Natasha responded almost immediately and we arranged to meet for coffee the next day after work. No sooner had we sat down with our drinks when Natasha began to speak about her Aunt and how she had raised her from a small child. As we were chatting I was taken to a house and as entered the house in my mind I was drawn to a very distinctive painting on the wall in the hallway. I described the painting to Natasha and asked her if it was of any significance to her, as at this stage I really had no idea whose house I was in! Natasha was virtually rendered speechless when she heard me describe house where she had been raised by her Aunt. To me it was a validation that I was on the right track and of course it gave Natasha confirmation that I wasn't a fraud. I asked her if she had any jewelry for me to read and she placed a small gold ring into the palm of my hand. Within seconds an image of a Jack Russell dog with a black patch over one eye appeared in my mind. Natasha confirmed the dog was a much loved family pet who had died many years earlier. The dog was sitting in a kitchen and a large wooden table was the main focal point in the room. I described this scene in detail to Natasha and again she agreed it was a very accurate description of the house she had lived in with her Aunt.

Other images were flashing quickly before me but nothing significant that I could share with Natasha when a voice called out to me the word aristocrats or so I thought and when I asked Natasha if it meant anything to me she looked at me blankly and told me she didn't have a clue what I was referring to. I was just about to admit defeat when I heard the word again only this time I realized it was not aristocrats but AristoCats as per the Disney film. When I corrected my mistake Natasha started to laugh and cry simultaneously and then she told me how AristoCats was in fact her Aunt's favorite film. Natasha admitted how emotional this had made her feel and had brought back many memories.

I asked Natasha if she or her family had any connection to gypsies in anyway but Natasha was unaware of any such association. I had a very strong sense that there was a connection of some sort but obviously a missing link can weaken the foundation when trying to establish such matters.

Nonetheless Natasha was very appreciative of the reading and how much comfort it had given her and also how many good memories it had brought back to her. It is very gratifying to receive such approval especially when you know it has helped someone when they are so obviously grief stricken.

A few weeks later Natasha asked me if I would be able to look at a photograph for her in to see if I could attain any information about any of the people in the photograph. Of course I agreed and she showed me a couple of old photographs. In the photograph there were 2 females and 1 male. Upon looking at the photograph I heard the name Bernadette and I also had a very negative feeling about the man in the photograph. I had a strong sense that this man could not be trusted and they should be wary of him. I related this information to Natasha who confirmed everything I had said about the photograph to be true.

I didn't ask Natasha what her reasons were for asking my opinion on the photograph, sometimes people what answers and it's not always necessary for the psychic to know what their questions are; for me it's just about helping people whenever I can, sharing the gift that has been bestowed upon me.

Natasha still comments on how accurate my readings have been for her and how much they helped her at a time in her life when she was despondent.

Paula has now moved back to the United Kingdom but we still keep in touch; both Natasha and Paula are waiting for their copies of this book, hopefully they enjoying reading it.

Chapter 36

We Are Still Here

I have mentioned previously that I have a wide circle of friends; some of whom believe in psychic mediumship and others who are skeptical. I would never let peoples personal opinions affect a friendship and at the same time I never try to inflict my beliefs onto any of my friends.

On occasions the level of psychic activity I experience can considerably diminish; this doesn't happen very often and I have no explanation for why it does happen but around this time I had not encountered any spiritual activity for several weeks.

So summer was upon us in our beautiful part of the world and a group of male friends and I were off on a lad's night out after a heavy week at work and enjoy a few beers in a local bar.

About 6 or 7 of us were meeting and we had only been in the bar for less than 15 minutes when we were putting the worlds to right as one often does on such occasions when quite suddenly I felt a sudden drop in energy around me, it only lasted for a second or two but it was very significant. As this had happened one of the bar staff had walked close by, I turned and watched her walk to the bar and just put it down to coincidence that she had walked past and ignored it. Approximately twenty minutes later she walked by again collecting glasses right next to our table and I had exactly the same feeling again it was very strange.

I gazed across at her in order to see if I could get any idea of what was going on; at this point I started to think that someone was eager for me to acknowledge the reason for now not yet known but of course my senses where on high alert and my interest strong.

When I concentrated on this lady she had an extremely negative and dark depressive aura, it was very overpowering and intense. I spoke to my friend Chris, who admittedly is quite skeptical in relation to all such matters, but discretely I pointed out this lady and said to him I'm not sure what is going on in her life but whatever it is she needs some help and I think someone is trying to get a message to her. He looked at me rather bemused and I gave him an account of what had just happened to me; I then told him if it happens a third time I would feel compelled to speak to her.

Needless to say the next time she was in my vicinity collecting glasses it happened a third time and as she headed back to the entrance of the bar, just as she got to the opened hatch I caught up with her.

It is always difficult making such an approach to complete strangers under these circumstances and no matter how compelling my need is to speak to them it's not an as easy as it sounds. So with some misgivings I quickly introduced myself and said to her what I'm about to say to you may sound bizarre but it is meant with good intention and I then told her that whatever was going on with her life at the moment it can only get better and she should aim to look forward. As expected the look on her face was one of disdain but I continued my quest and said to her I'm sure you must think I'm crazy but she should really listen to me as I was genuinely only concerned about her well-being and I asked her to take a minute to hear me out.

At that point she started crying and it did appear that there was obviously something concerning her. We walked across to a quieter part of the bar and she asked me how I knew she was feeling this way and I told her a little bit about myself. I advised her that no matter what difficulties we are experiencing in life they will always improve however I was fully aware that when people feel down they can quickly spiral into depression and sometimes people need a little nudge in the right direction, some guidance or just words of reassurance that there is light at the end of the tunnel. She confirmed to me she had been feeling very flat and disheartened, she didn't elaborate any further and not wishing to intrude I just tried to reassure her that this time would pass.

Our discussion lasted only a few minutes and I returned to my friends. Chris asked what had happened and I said I had just passed on my thoughts to her and he said at least I tried, which I suppose was true but I still felt my conversation with her had been left unresolved.

I noticed her several more times as the evening continued and I could still see a dark aura around her. I then asked spirit who is pushing through as I need to tell her a name, next minute the words Peter, Peter, Peter were literally shouted at me. I thought finally I was making progress!! Not holding back I walked up to her and said I know who it is who is looking out for you it's Peter. Once again I received that look of disdain and she dismissed me instantly and said no you're wrong I don't know anyone called Peter. I asked her to have a think about it as on occasion people cannot recall a name at first, she acknowledged this and walked away.

I went back to Chris and told him what happened and he too didn't seem too impressed as she didn't recognize the name, maybe it just wasn't my night and it was me who was way off the mark.

A couple of minutes later I felt a tap on my shoulder and turned to see the barmaid standing behind me, she asked me for a quick word. I moved over to one of the booths and I sat down across from her, she then told me she did know Peter it was her grandfather who had recently passed away. She had not associated the name with him as no-one ever called him by that name and now she felt guilty for not making the connection to her grandfather. I advised her not to feel this way, it wouldn't be what her grandfather would want. When a loved one passes away they will come back and give you a special sign often to let you know they are safe but also to support and comfort the loved ones they have left behind and I was confident this was indeed her grandfather's intention and she should seek comfort from this.

It was his way of pushing through to put his arms around her as a wonderful gesture of love and support just when she needed it. Understandably she became quite emotional again but she seemed as though a weight had been lifted from her shoulders and her relief was obvious. She apologized to me for being abrupt and thanked me for approaching her and giving her a message from her much loved grandfather. I now felt that my message had been delivered and I was happy with the outcome. I wished her well and one again returned to my friends.

When I told Chris what had transpired he was genuinely impressed and congratulated me for being so unwavering in my beliefs and ensuring that this lady connected with her grandfather.

For the first time that evening I enjoyed a beer and I felt content the next time the lady walked by me and I could see a noticeable difference as she was collecting glasses, her aura was visibly brighter and I could see a difference in her whole persona.

Chapter 37

Meditation without Wings

The Psychic Nerd

A common theme that many people in the psychic community advised me to practice was meditation and with this in mind I finally made a point to look for classes near home.

I was introduced by a mutual friend to a lady called Marie who conducted open meditation groups on a weekly basis. As soon as I met Marie I felt a tremendous welcoming and warm feeling around her and I knew that it had been inevitable that our paths would cross; from that point that I had no hesitation about attending her future meditation classes. When Marie and I met we hit it off immediately and were soon comparing stories and experiences though my skills and knowledge paled in comparison to hers I hoped to learn as much from her as possible.

I arrived at my first session which was held at a converted outdoor building in her garden. The environment was as you would expect, very calming, with candles burning, music playing softly in the background and large cushions and bean bags scattered on the floor.

There were seven of us in total, both male and female of all different ages. I took a seat near the far side against the wall. We were asked to remove our shoes no watches were permitted during meditation. The art of meditation is timeless hence the rule of no watches and when you think about it our lives are dictated by time so in order to truly meditate time must not be a concern. Now that I was prepared for my first experience I was rather looking forward to having a period of reflection and contemplation without the usual time constraints that we live by every hour of every day.

We commenced the meditation with deep breathing exercises and Marie spoke softly about surrounding ourselves with white light. Following her instruction I pictured myself with a white light emerging from the top of my head and flowing down my body to form a protective bubble around me.

Marie described to us about different breathing techniques and how important it was to identify your breathing travelling through your body until you feel as though you are connecting with mother earth. This may seem like a strange analogy however when you are in the full throes of meditation the final stages of connecting with mother earth can be remarkable.

Prior to starting my meditation for some unknown reason I had been somewhat apprehensive and when starting my meditation I soon realized that subconsciously I was putting up barriers and I tried my best to follow Marie's advice to assist me in removing these barriers. After several attempts I finally perfected my breathing and the results were phenomenal.

Marie then described to us how next we were going to envision ourselves lifted in the air as though we had no boundaries. As soon as she said no boundaries I just felt myself taking off like a rocket and as Marie continued with her instructions she then told us to imagine looking from high above, sitting in a large tree surveying the fields below. I on the other hand had visualized myself in space looking down at the planet earth far below me and I instantly realized I had gone too fast, too far and had to picture myself back in the tree.

In my meditative state I returned to earth and find a tree when Marie then asked us to imagine before us large fields with lovely green pastures but the fields in my mind were all colored gold and firstly I was floating and then flying across the fields with my fingertips slightly touching the blades of grass.

At this moment all I could feel was total relaxation and I could feel and hear everything; when people use the expression listening to the grass grow this was how I would imagine it to be it was so peaceful. I seemed to continue in this phase for what felt like hours when Marie gradually brought us back to normality releasing our connections to the earth and eventually returning us to our pre-meditation state.

We then sat together as a group to discuss our personal experiences. It was extremely interesting listening to each person's individual accounts and how different each one was. It came to me and I told them all about how I found myself looking over my shoulder and could see the earth as the size of a drawing pin. As I was telling them this Marie told me that she had noted within the meditation go very deep very quickly and what I described totally explained that; she was amazed metaphorically at how far I had travelled.

It was quite surprising to hear this but admittedly I had thoroughly enjoyed my first meditation experience and was looking forward to my next one.

The following week at my next session we again started with the light protection then connected to the earth but little did I know my second attempt at meditation would surpass the previous experience.

This time Marie took us to a wonderful place full of white light with such a warm feeling of love it was overpowering. She then described to us how a presence or feeling would appear to our side and a hand would be reached out towards us, we were told to place our hand onto the hand. Following her instruction I placed my hand out in front of me and I could feel such a powerful energy surging through my body at a phenomenal rate. What happened next was a total shock as another hand appeared to my other side and I looked down and placed my free hand onto it. The energy flowing through my body had now increased two fold, I felt like I could hold onto these hands forever.

As I mentioned earlier time is irrelevant when meditating and I have no idea how long I was in this state but at some point Marie began to tell us that the hand was starting to move away and we should gradually start to float back down to earth until we eventually arrived back again to the meditation room.

When I did come back I slowly began to open my eyes and do some stretches as Marie suggested and I felt such profound tranquility it's difficult to describe how intense it was, it was how I would imagine coming out of hibernation felt like.

Again we discussed what happened as a group, Marie informed us that the hand we had connected with were our individual spirit guides and immediately asked if anybody was given a name. I told them how two hands had appeared to me and I tried to share with them the intensity of the power and force of energy was something I have never experienced before in my lifetime. Unfortunately I was not given the name of my guides; this is one thing I would like to determine even now but a name has never come through to me.

My third session and final was just as interesting as the previous two. In this final meditation class Marie requested when we connected with the earth that we imagine a skyline at night. In the first instance I was standing on a hillside overlooking a really modern skyline with skyscrapers and modern buildings made of glass with many of the buildings lit up but I didn't recognize where this place was. Marie then instructed us to float upwards away from the skyline and move to another location. Within a few seconds I found myself floating between two Egyptian pyramids holding a large staff in my right hand; it was night time and I could clearly see flame lit torches burning brightly and lighting up the buildings below me and there were people moving around. All these people were dressed in ancient Egyptian costumes and as I looked down I too was dressed this way.

Marie then told us to lift up again, at which point I began to flying over the middle east before heading towards Norway/Sweden where I only appeared to stay for a couple of seconds before flying off again but this time felt myself flying across Iceland and coming down into a crescent path to the far north of the United States, I would say it was probably more in the Canadian area however it was hard to tell. It was all very surreal and it was amazing how my mind was transporting me to all these places. As the session drew to a close once again I was astounded by what had taken place it was all very surreal and it certainly did set me on the path to practice meditation.

I meditate on occasions when I find I need too, however in my opinion I should do a lot more than I do at the moment. Strangely enough one of the best places I find to meditate is on a crowded train during my daily commute, people just see you like everyone else with headphones on and don't realize you are relaxing in your own little world and not just listening to music its very therapeutic.

Chapter 38

Positive Uses

The Psychic Nerd

I often wonder why I have experienced all I have since I was a child; it's certainly no ordinary life. I think to myself why can I do these things and in what positive ways could I use them for. I believe that what I have is a gift which I should use for the good of others. The events included in this chapter are the types of experiences my skills could be used for in a very positive manner.

The first experience occurred approximately two years ago around April 2012; Helen had been watching the news on CNN and asked me if I heard the very sad news about a little girl who had disappeared from her bedroom at home. I will not mention the little girl's name however she lived in the Arizona area of the United States. I asked Helen to let me know the news story was repeated which she did and when I looked at the photograph of this little girl there was something about her which just grabbed my attention and after hearing the story I just could not get the image of her smiling face out of my head.

Unfortunately these stories are all too common and sadly children disappear everyday across the world, but for some unknown reason several hours later I just kept seeing her little smiling face. Rather than just dismissing this I began to concentrate intently on her face and I started to build up a mental picture of an old building similar to a barn but not as large and it was surrounded by a long grassy area, the whole area looked overgrown and disused and there was a stream running alongside it. Outside of the building was a rather distinctive metal pole which appeared to be old and rusted. The surrounding area seemed swampy or marsh-like in appearance. As the images were coming into my mind it was so clear that I sketched it onto some paper.

The next evening a further news report came on about her disappearance and the footage showed the area behind her house where she was last seen. As soon as I saw her house a picture of white gloves, similar to industrial gloves, and I could see them near my head coming towards me. The next image was of an old 4x4 vehicle dark green in color with no cover on the back being driven away from the house and it was travelling very slowly. In my mind I could see the path the 4x4 was taking and a few notable landmarks appeared to me and then the imaged faded away. Again I made a note of what I had seen, I don't know why.

A couple of days had passed and I was sitting on the train commuting to work in Perth when the little girl's face once again appeared in my mind; this had been happening on numerous occasions since I had initially heard about her disappearance. It was disconcerting to say the least and as you can appreciate with my past history I was concerned as to why I was receiving these images.

I made the conscious decision to try my best and use my ability to find out more so upon arriving at work I went directly to my office and decided to do just that, there was no time to waste.

The sketch I had drawn was in my brief case, I took it out and with the sketch before me and the few notes I had written down I tried to focus on all these details in conjunction with the image of the little girl as I needed something more significant to go on. Concentrating intently I heard the words I73, it was repeated to me on a couple of occasions quite deliberately spelt out I 7 3 and I had absolutely no idea what this could relate to.

At a loss to know what this meant I searched on Google for I73 and nothing that I could associate with this missing girl turned up in the search engine results. I tried another few searches with the same results and I then tried I73 Tucson which was the region in Arizona connected to the disappearance and I was stunned to see a story about I-73 or interstate 73 which was intended for construction and there had been recent protestors complaining about wetlands being destroyed to make way for interstate 73.

It sent shivers down my spine when I read the full article and on looking at the pictures in the article it was very similar to what I had drawn and I had made a note of the area being marsh-like or swampy.

Now just to clarify I have never been to Arizona before in my life or anywhere close by. I didn't have a clue about I-73 until this moment in time, and likewise I was unaware that there were wetlands in this area. To me this information was a credible validation and I now had to decide to do with it.

Should I send this information to the local police department in Arizona or do nothing at all? Despite believing my facts to be credible I was also aware how police are bombarded with a huge assortment of witnesses many of whom are not always reliable sources and I didn't want to waste their time if my specifics were incorrect.

I rang Helen to seek her advice as she is always levelheaded and I can always rely on her to be objective. Helen advised me to email everything I knew to the Arizona Police Department, at least then it was up to the investigating team to decide to use this information or not and by doing this I had done as much as possible.

I done just that, I sent an email to the local police department first asking them not to ignore my email as a crank and then laid out the facts as I have told in this chapter, I even sent a copy of the sketch I had drawn. I did receive a formal acknowledgement of the email and an assurance that all items of information would be considered which did make me feel as though I had done the right thing.

Unfortunately, to date at the time of completing this book in November 2014 this little girl was still missing but I hope and pray that one day she may return safely to her family.

The second event occurred in October 2012 and the scenario was very similar; another little girl had gone missing in the UK, only this time it seemed apparent almost from the start that she had been abducted whilst playing near her home after school.

As soon as I saw the photograph of this young girl I immediately visualized myself standing in front of a very white/sky blue colored outhouse or building. The roof of the building was made of old grey slate and I was standing approximately 3 feet away from the door. The building also had a small square window to the left. I would say in size the building was no more than 12 foot in length. The area was very rural but apart from this I did not pick up any significant landmarks which might assist in locating this building.

The speed at which I was transported to this location was quite disconcerting but I instantly knew wherever I was had to be connected to the abduction of this little girl. I kept hearing her name repeatedly in my head and then as quickly as it had appeared it had gone. For several days I tried to reconnect with what I had previously seen but unfortunately I was unsuccessful.

Regardless of this fact I still felt obliged to send an email to the police authority dealing with this abduction and they responded by saying they would certainly look into the information I had sent to them.

Regrettably this case did not end well and a man was later charged and found guilty of the abduction and murder of this little girl. I can only hope she is now at peace after having her life ended so tragically young.

In relation to both of these experiences I can totally understand how the police must be inundated with similar offers of help hopefully by many genuine psychics but also by some impostors too so it is difficult to know how they are perceived by the police. However I do know that several police departments use psychics on a regular basis and it is no secret that these psychics, working in conjunction with the police, have helped solved many murder cases. A truly inspiring way of using your psychic ability for the greater good.

Chapter 39

Tower of London

The Psychic Nerd

In April 2013 as a family we went back to United Kingdom on holiday for a month. During this trip we spent a week in a hotel in London and all 3 of us had a wonderful time visiting all the well know tourist destinations. Both Helen and I had visited the capital on numerous occasions but Lucas had only been a young boy on our last visit and didn't really remember much about it so with this in mind it was our intention to be fully fledged tourists for the week. We had a list of tourist attractions we all wanted to visit and by far the top of my list was the Tower of London as despite visiting London many times before I had never ever visited the Tower of London.

On the day of our visit we arrived early and purchased our tickets and I must admit knowing a little about the gruesome history of the Tower I was hopeful that I might pick up on something as we were walking around so I commenced the tour with high expectations.

We walked around all the walls on the outside of the Tower which had originally formed the outer part of the fortress when it was built near the start of the 11th century. It truly was fascinating just walking around trying to take in the magnitude of the many historical events that must have occurred here over the years.

It was interesting to learn how the Tower had evolved over the years and hearing about the torture and executions that had taken place there I was certain there would be something lurking around that I would pick up on but I sensed absolutely nothing.

We then continued our tour to The White Tower which is the oldest part of the Tower of London and was apparently built to cause fear to the uncontrollable citizens of London. Indeed from the outside it is very imposing standing approximately 90 feet high and it is made up of 3 floors where apparently the basement was used to torture and interrogate prisoners. Over the centuries the White Tower has been a fortress, a palace and a prison and when we entered it I was surprised at how it was laid out. To be honest I actually expected an assortment of smaller rooms and I was very surprised to see how open plan it was.

As we were walking around yet again I did not pick up on anything though I must admit I was in awe of the whole experience it was fascinating just to have the privilege of being in such a historical place. We then entered the chapel; Helen and Lucas were a few steps ahead of me and no sooner had I walked into the chapel and crossed the threshold when a male figure ran towards and grabbed hold of my left arm. He had a very peculiar dark colored hair and he was dressed in period clothing. The force of his hands grabbing my arm was considerable, he did not speak to me but just held onto me for approximately 20 seconds. I didn't try to shake him off, I felt remarkably calm and we just stood staring at each other and then he was gone. I looked around to see if anyone had witnessed what had happened but no-one appeared to have done so.

I walked quickly to catch up with Helen and recounted to her what had just happened to me. She jokingly exclaimed that she was surprised it had taken me that long!! I looked around the chapel to see if I could see this figure again but there was no trace of him.

The rest of the tour was uneventful and I must admit all 3 of us thoroughly enjoyed our visit to the Tower of London; perhaps for different reasons, but a good day was had by all nonetheless.

Chapter 40

Coffee Confirmation

The Psychic Nerd

Earlier in this book I mentioned that I have periods in my life when I have a lull in the level of spiritual activity I experience. Leading into this story I was rather disillusioned with the path my career was taking at this stage and I was trying my hardest to make changes for the better.

When I work in the CBD (Central Business District) in Perth I regularly visit a little café on Barrack Street, it is my little bolt-hole where I can escape the pressures and demands of work, enjoy an excellent coffee and some much needed peace and quiet. One of the ladies who works there is called Carol she is very friendly and always happy to have chat and she makes amazing coffee too.

Once after I was in the café having a coffee and reading the paper when I had noticed Carol talking to another customer, nothing odd about that of course but there was just something about this lady that grabbed my attention. I didn't pick up on anything but as I said my senses were low so I put it down to that.

About a week or so later I returned to the café and Carol was working together with the lady who owned the café. They were both standing next to the counter as I entered they both said hello and I placed my usual order. We chatted away and then bearing in my I have been visiting this café for several years, Carol out of the blue asked me what my occupation was; strangely enough before she had even asked me the question I knew that she was going to. I told her I worked in the I.T. industry and I designed computer systems and she smiled at me and said what about the other skills you have.

I asked her why she was asking me and she began to tell me about her friend who had been in the café. Before she could go any further I interrupted and asked if this was the lady who had been in the café the previous week last week and I gave her a description; she confirmed it was the same person. Carol then told me that her friend had noticed me and she had mentioned to Carol that I was spiritually gifted and I had spirits around me all the time. Now to hear this at a time when I was experiencing a low activity in my psychic awareness was quite a revelation.

I then told Carol a little about the psychic side of me and she asked if I could give her a reading. I agreed and we sat at a table together and as I often do I asked for a piece of her jewelry and closed the jewelry in my palm.

The Psychic Nerd

Now as I held this jewelry I didn't really expect to receive a great deal, if anything at all, however as soon as I held it I could see the image of a little girl playing in a garden. She was looking directly at me smiling and she had beautiful blonde hair. Her image stayed with me for quite some time and she was constantly running around, playing and smiling. I described her to Carol who in turn told me than whenever she has visited a psychic over the years they have all described this young girl, always with the beautiful blonde hair and smiling face. Carol informed me many years earlier she had lost a little girl during child birth and she was convinced this was who was always with her and I totally agreed with her. She took comfort in the fact that even after all this time her little girl was still around and always appeared happy.

I must admit I was pleasantly surprised to have given Carol such accurate information especially at the time when my spiritual activity was low. It never ceases to amaze me how the spirits always find ways of just giving you that nudge in the right direction when you need it.

Chapter 41

Family Comes Calling

In March of 2012 my Father passed after battling cancer for several years. Unfortunately due to an assortment of family issues and fallouts I had not seen him for the last eight years of his life.

On reflection I know that the length of time the majority of my family has been estranged is very sad for us all; we were once very close knit but I am sad to many of us have been divided for too many years. We often get too caught up in squabbles and disagreements and before you know it years have passed us all by and it is very difficult to re-establish that connection no matter how hard you try. All our children have grown up strangers to their extended family who they have never met and have missed out on an abundance of family relationships throughout their childhood and unfortunately will continue to do so if the situation does not change.

After I had heard the news about my Father's passing I was of course upset and sad for a whole number of reasons, none more so than for the length of time we had been estranged and now it was too late to do anything about it.

Several months after my Father had died I was at home, fast asleep only to wake up in the middle for no particular reason, or so I thought.

In our bedroom opposite the bed we have a seating area, a quiet area that I often use to meditate or Helen likes to sit and read there, and I must admit it is a favorite spot of mine at home.

So back to being woken from my sleep, as I began to stir I immediately sensed a presence in the room. I gently sat up so as not to disturb Helen and there sitting in this area as though they had just called in for a cup of tea was not only my Father but also his Mum, by beloved Nan.

I crept out of bed and walked across the room to both of them and as I did I felt something brush past my legs. I looked down and there at my feet was our beautiful boxer dog Tasha, who had passed several years earlier, she was moving in and out of my legs, wagging her tail which was always her way of greeting us.

I looked at Tasha and then back to my Nan and before I had a chance to say anything my Father stood up from the chair and walked towards me, he then put his arms around me and gave me a hug. We both just stood there and neither of us uttered a word. We gradually moved apart and I turned to my Nan and to this day I have no idea why I said it out of all the things I could have told her, I just said your favorite color is blue. She looked at me, smiled and before I had a chance to speak to them, ask them both a million and one questions that now sprang to my mind, my Dad, Nan and Tasha just faded away before me. I stood still just staring at where they had been moments earlier and I felt as though I had lost them all over again, and if I am perfectly honest with myself I had never truly mourned the loss of my Dad until that night. It then hit me that in this life we would never have the opportunity to put things right it was too late for that but it gave me hope that we would be reconciled at some point in time.

Finally I went back to bed and I just lay awake trying to make sense of what had just happened. From my perspective I think it was my Dad's way of telling me he too was sorry for what had happened between us and perhaps the presence of my Nan and my dog Tasha was his way of showing me that our family would one day be reunited. I think he was also re-establishing a connection with me that had been broken for far too long.

For the rest of the night I slept like a log and when Helen woke up in the morning I turned to her and said you'll never believe who visited me in the night!!

Chapter 42

What are you waiting for

The Psychic Nerd

I have already mentioned a part of this story in the very early chapters of this book. This was the last visit I actually had to my local spiritualist church and it would certainly become a memorable one.

When I arrived Nicky was again present and she was seated at the front next to a lady who I did not know. The session started and after about fifteen minutes this lady stood up and straight away started to head in my direction before stopping directly in front of me. Not once did she hesitate about who she was looking for and she then pointed right at me and announced that she wanted to speak to me about an older male figure who is coming through. Now I am only in my 40's so there was a good chance my parents could still be alive but she said I have your father here in spirit.

She gave a very accurate description of my father, who incidentally I do not resemble, and she then began a truthful account of how problematic our relationship had been when he was alive and how regretful he was of this and he wished he could have made amends before he passed. I remained passive in my chair, not wanting to give anything away but I was rather impressed with what she was telling me. He told her how proud he was of my success, which was something he had never told me before, and he added that on occasions however I am my own worst enemy.

The psychic asked me if I knew what this meant and I nodded that I did. She continued then by telling me that I could achieve a lot more if only I stopped doubting and holding myself back.

This is what the reference to being my own worst enemy related to and I must admit I had to agree with this 100%. She continued on by saying that my Father was telling her that I needed to have the confidence in the ideas I come up with rather than developing them and not taking it any further as these ideas could lead to a change for the better in the future for myself and my family. He told me not to live a life of regrets as he had often done and he knew I had the courage to move forward and he would be with me every step of the way with his hand on my shoulder pushing me forward.

She was drawing to a conclusion and then she asked me had I been undecided about attending the meeting this evening which I had been but had a change of heart at the last minute and decided to attend, before I answered she told me that was the first, gentle push in the right direction from my Dad – he had to get me there somehow!

Every single thing she had told me was correct, talk about validation and as I had discussed in an earlier chapter about the health problems I had experienced a year earlier, the gloves were off and after this message from my Father I was coming out of my corner like a raging bull.

After the meeting it felt so good to have received such a precise reading and as I got in my car to drive home I felt unstoppable and I decided at that moment that I would devise a plan to develop all my ideas, starting with writing this book and lo and behold within 6 months of putting pen to paper it was complete with the occasional push from my Dad of course.

Chapter 43

Crayons

The Psychic Nerd

The time is now March 2014 and this chapter is probably one of the last in the book but it is as relevant to me as every other chapter in this book. If I have ever wondered why I have my skills, and I can assure you I have many times, the events of this evening definitely answered a few questions.

One Saturday evening Helen and I had invited some of our friends over for dinner and drinks. As is often the case on such occasions, people splinter off into smaller groups and I found myself in the kitchen talking to couple called Susie and Paul.

Susie and Paul have two beautiful little daughters both under the age of four years and very sadly they had lost their first child, a little boy, due to complications when he was born. Susie knew about my spiritual skills and she began talking to me about how guilty she felt at times for not always thinking about her little boy as her life was so busy being a full-time mum to two toddlers, which obviously was very demanding plus the fact that she also ran a successful business from home and took care of her running her household, it was no surprise that she didn't think about him every moment.

I tried to reassure her by telling her that she had nothing to feel guilty about and probably thought about him subconsciously throughout the day without even realizing.

I also told her that her little boy would be around her all the time she just probably wasn't aware of it. I honestly believe that the second you think of a family member who has passed their presence is immediately near or around you.

As I was explaining this to Susie and Paul I heard someone saying to me green crayons which meant absolutely nothing to me and I tried to ignore it and continued talking. Whoever was telling me this did not want to be ignored and they were speaking in an adult voice and extremely clearly saying green crayons another 3 or 4 times until I could ignore it no longer.

I stopped what I was talking about and said to Susie and Paul I think I have a message for you both, I have been asked to tell you about the green crayons. As soon as I said this Susie raised her hand to her mouth and just said oh my god. She looked at Paul and they both looked at me before Paul explained that one of their daughters loved green crayons and they were always finding them discarded around the house but more recently they have been finding green crayon drawings all over the house on walls and surfaces and they did not know who was putting them there. They had both initially thought it was one of their daughters but many of the drawings were appearing in places that they could not possibly reach and even in rooms that they had no access too,

As soon as they informed me of this everything started to click into place and I was certain it was their little boy making his presence known throughout the home by making these markings in various places.

I advised them that the next time they noticed any of these green crayon markings they should just take a moment to acknowledge their little boy as it was his way of letting them know he was always around them and he was ok.

Chapter 44

General Beliefs

I thought I would add this chapter to just give a greater insight into some of my general beliefs. I have stated many times in this book I have over 30 years of analysis and design experience in the I.T. industry and it is this logic that I apply to all aspects of my life including my spirituality. I am not the sort of person who believes everything I read or hear; I try to look at everything objectively and logically before I form my own opinion.

On the subject of religion I am not religious at all, I was christened Church of England and attended church with my parents until about the age of 11. I do believe that children should have guidance from a faith of whatever denomination but they should be allowed their own choice once old enough to do so. Our son was christened and raised a Catholic as was Helen and her family are quite religious which I totally respect and it has never been an issue between us.

Whenever I walk into any Church, regardless of the denomination, I can assure you there is a strong spiritual presence in every one. There is an energy that surrounds me and trust me when I tell you I feel it every time I find myself in a church. Although I said I am not religious I do believe in

God, a higher power, I just do not conform to one particular religion.

I feel very sad when I hear of extremists or terrorists using religion to justify the killing of innocent people worldwide and such practices I am sure would not be condoned by any God.

I have a keen interest in all things spiritual and supernatural and really enjoy a good horror movie, although Helen usually sits next to me in the theatre room hidden behind as many cushions as she can find, well they do say opposites attract and we have been together for almost 25 years now and are still going strong, I definitely found my soul mate and knew it from the moment I set eyes on her.

When you have experienced what I have over the years you tend to look at life quite differently, you don't just take things for what they are or appear to be. You ask questions, investigate, learn and evolve.

One area that fascinates me is the subject of the UFO phenomenon, personally I think a lot of what we hear is not accurate but there is always that small percentage that makes you think again.

Just take a look up into the clear dark sky at night, the billions of stars you see, logically how can we possibly expect to be the only living beings in the universe?

If you read this book and you are one of the people like I used to be who chose to be a victim and take what life gives them I hope this book may make you realize you can change.

I hear too many accounts of tragedy in peoples' lives we only get one life, live yours to the utmost without regret.

I had an idea to write a book and I am certainly not an accomplished writer and I am sure it is a little rough around the edges but who knows what will come of it but I've done it and will never regret doing so.

Chapter 45

Where to Now

Now that I have finished my book I have plans to attend some psychic development classes which I hope will enable me to enhance my skills and use them to their maximum potential as currently I am sure I am only tapping into a small volume of what is available to me.

Writing this book has been a very cathartic experience for me despite bringing up many deep rooted memories from my childhood that still to this day send shivers down my spine it has been good to put these memories down on paper.

I have spent many weekends and late nights writing this book and on many occasions I have not been alone, I have often sensed spirits looking over my shoulder and when I turn around there is no-one there, something I'm sure we all experience from time to time. Don't be afraid, they are just passing through and mean no harm.

Who knows where my journey will take me following the publication of this book all I hope is that Helen and Lucas will continue to take that journey with me.

The final message to you is ……………

It's all a true story and is not an ordinary life......

www.ingramcontent.com/pod-product-compliance
Lightning Source LLC
Chambersburg PA
CBHW071854290426
44110CB00013B/1141